Praying Luther's Small Catechism

The Pattern of Sound Words

John T. Pless

CONCORDIA PUBLISHING HOUSE · SAINT LOUIS

For the Rev. Dr. Norman E. Nagel on the occasion of his 90th birthday.

Published by Concordia Publishing House
3558 S. Jefferson Ave., St. Louis, MO 63118–3968
1-800-325-3040 • www.cph.org

Library of Congress Cataloging-in-Publication Data

Names: Pless, John T., 1953- author.
Title: Praying Luther's Small catechism : the pattern of sound words / John T. Pless.
Description: St. Louis : Concordia Publishing House, 2016. | Includes bibliographical references.
Identifiers: LCCN 2015049726 (print) | LCCN 2016020755 (ebook) | ISBN 9780758654823 | ISBN 9780758654830
Subjects: LCSH: Luther, Martin, 1483-1546. Kleine Katechismus. | Lutheran Church--Catechisms. | Theology, Doctrinal--Popular works. | Devotional literature.
Classification: LCC BX8070.L8 P54 2016 (print) | LCC BX8070.L8 (ebook) | DDC 238/.41--dc23
LC record available at https://lccn.loc.gov/2015049726

1   2   3   4   5   6   7   8   9   10   25   24   23   22   21   20   19   18   17   16

Table of Contents

Abbreviations

AE	Luther's Works; American Edition
FC	Formula of Concord
FC Ep	Epitome of the Formula of Concord
K-W	*The Book of Concord*; edited by Robert Kolb and Timothy J. Wengert
LC	Large Catechism
LSB	*Lutheran Service Book*
SA	Smalcald Articles
SC	Small Catechism
SD	Solid Declaration of the Formula of Concord

Foreword

In the Lutheran Church, Luther's catechisms became formative for Christian instruction. Over the centuries, the Small Catechism in particular has been taught and learned by heart in confirmation classes around the world. In this way, not only education in pivotal articles of Christian faith took place but also the mind-sets of Lutheran congregants have been shaped over generations. Moreover, Lutheran piety has been coined in such a manner that Lutherans may be recognized and distinguished by the way they talk about God, venerate their Savior, Jesus Christ, as their Lord, and show how they are guided by the Holy Spirit. John Pless deserves to be given credit for having rediscovered and now for highlighting Luther's idea of *praying* the catechism.

The inner structure of Luther's catechisms is guided by the idea of God's solemn and sacred self-communication. This leitmotif steers the explanation of the Ten Commandments, as the First Commandment is focused on God's promise: "I, I myself will give you what you need and help you out of every danger." To this promise, God's claim corresponds: "Only do not let your heart cling to or rest in anyone else."[1] In the First Article of the Creed, Luther states "The Father has given to us himself with all creation . . . apart from the fact that he has also showered us with inexpressible eternal blessings through his Son and the Holy Spirit."[2] Thus, in the Second Article, we learn how God "has given himself completely to us, withholding nothing."[3] So the Creed helps "us do what the Ten Commandments require of us."[4] The petitions in Lord's Prayer, correspondingly, request nothing else but the fulfillment of what is commanded in the Decalogue;[5] moreover, "God takes the initiative and puts into our mouths the very words."[6] Likewise, the Sacraments are regarded as "a treasure that God gives us and faith grasps,"[7] or "all the treasures he brought from heaven for us," "placed at everyone's door, yes upon the table."[8]

---

1   LC I 4; K-W 387.

2   LC II 24; K-W 433.

3   LC II 26; K-W 434.

4   LC II 2; K-W 431.

5   K-W 440ff.

6   LC III 22; K-W 443.

7   LC IV 37; K-W 461.

8   LC V 66, 35; K-W 473, 470.

For the Lutheran Church—and even beyond—Luther became instrumental with his catechisms in presenting the Christian community with an introduction to a life guided by God.[9] He points out that Holy Baptism is God's salutary self-communication, which brings to us "God's grace, the entire Christ, and the Holy Spirit with his gifts"[10] He views the Sacrament of the Altar, as "this great . . . treasure, which is daily administered and distributed among Christians," providing the new human being with constant fortification in his battle against Satan, death, and sin.[11] The Lord's Prayer invokes God's irrefutable willingness for mercy in just such a battle, a battle that becomes inevitable for a Christian. It is precisely when a Christian partakes in God's self-giving and self-revelation, that a Christian takes on his enemies in the battle of the Gospel for the Gospel.[12]

Luther can be perceived as being the one who construes the Credo for us, thereby gratefully accepting "what God does for us and gives to us"[13] and the implementation thereof in the reality of Christ's liberation act, since Christ "has brought us back from the devil to God, from death to life, from sin to righteousness, and keeps us there."[14] It is Luther who substantiates the identity of Christianity and Church as being trinitarian, and who identifies the Christocentric aspect as being a distinctive feature of Christendom and Christianity, compared to all other forms of religiosity (and a-religiosity) that are not based on Christ or inspired by the Holy Spirit.[15]

It is Luther who is able to discern Law and Gospel as being God's immanent manner of speaking and acting[16] in which the gradient from the "extrinsic"—or even "alien"—to the "actual"—rather, "proper"—work of God proceeds in such a way[17] that the Church must never be found wanting in proclaiming the declaration of forgiveness and the salvation in Christ, seeing that it is a matter of "comforting and consoling" those who are frightened and "fainthearted."[18]

---

9   Cf. Werner Klän, "*Anleitung zu einem Gott-gelenkten Leben. Die innere Systematic der Katechismen Luthers*," *Lutherische Theologie und Kirche* 29 (2005): 18–35.

10   LC IV 42; K-W 461.

11   K-W 470ff.

12   K-W 448ff.; 451.

13   LC II 67; K-W 440.

14   LC II 31; K-W 434.

15   K-W 440.

16   Cf. the citations from Luther's exegesis of Luke 5:1–11 in the summer homily of 1544, in FC SD V 12; K-W 583ff.

17   K-W 585 ff.

18   FC SD V 12; K-W 584.

It is Luther who places the Gospel in its forms of implementation—proclamation, Baptism, Eucharist, and confessional penitence as the "third sacrament"[19]—at the center of an encompassing Christian understanding of a worship service.[20] It is Luther who, by the differentiation of the two realms,[21] the release of secularism from clerical paternalism, as well as the theological facilitation of the differentiation between "penultimate" and "ultimate," thereby paves the way for the separation of church and state—yet without ever having relinquished God's reign of power over all ages, nations, people, and spheres of life.[22]

It is Luther who, by the end of his Large Catechism, urged the Christian community of solidarity to bear in mind that we "must all help us to believe, to love, *to pray*, and to fight against the devil,"[23] meaning the elementary and fundamental day-to-day life of a Christian existence. Indeed, all five parts of Luther's catechisms, linked to one another by the principle of God's self-donation willing to communicate His salvation to all humankind, are meant to be effective as an introduction to fundamental consummations of Christian life, even on a "daily" basis.[24]

With this perspective in mind, praying the catechism serves as an exemplary piece of Christian piety and a strong impulse to formatting Christian life in the light of the Gospel as rediscovered in the Lutheran Reformation. The catechism must be taught in the Church, on all accounts. It ought to be learned, definitely, although—or even because—we observe that in many a Western country the ability of memorizing texts is in decline. The catechism has to be preached, as it comprises the sound doctrine of the Church. Therefore, it may be meditated on as well. But first and foremost the catechism is meant to be *prayed*, as a daily exercise, as Luther wished it to be. John Pless, in his comprehensive analysis, directs our attention to exercising and cultivating our Christian existence on a daily basis by advising us—along the lines of Luther's catechetical instruction—to engage in the lifelong practice of being a Christian.

Werner Klän
Oberursel/Germany
Reformation Day 2015

---

19   K-W 465.

20   K-W 319.

21   K-W 470ff.

22   K-W 389, 451.

23   LC V 87; K-W 476.

24   K-W 431, 444, 466, 469.

Preface

Edmund Schlink spoke of modernity as that time when dogmatics had become largely a playground for the subjective originality of speculative piety, a period in which Christians generally forgot how to pray through their catechism. Schlink's words call us back to something that ought to characterize Lutherans. Namely, both pastors and laypeople should remember how to "pray through their catechism," for it tutors us in what Paul calls the "pattern of sound words," locating us within the economy of God's giving and our receiving. The Small Catechism guides us into the heart of the Holy Scriptures, for it is, as the Formula of Concord would come to call it, "a Bible of the Laity, in which everything is summarized that is treated in detail in Holy Scripture and that is necessary for a Christian to know for salvation."[25] The apostle Paul charges Timothy to "follow the pattern of the sound words . . . in the faith and love that are in Christ Jesus" (2 Timothy 1:13). The Small Catechism is such a pattern. Hence the title of this book— *Praying Luther's Small Catechism: The Pattern of Sound Words.*

I have come to appreciate what Oswald Bayer calls "catechetical systematics" as an approach for doing Lutheran theology. This book was conceived and crafted with Bayer's description in mind. The catechism provides both the categories and contours of our theology. Even as the catechism functioned as a handbook of doctrine, so it also served as prayer book in the Reformation. Luther was of the conviction that the catechism could be prayed. This book that you now hold in your hands might be thought of as an exercise in prayed dogmatics. I have benefited greatly from the recently translated five-volume study of Albrecht Peters, *Commentary on Luther's Catechisms.* By publishing Peters's work, Concordia Publishing House has given the English-speaking Lutheran world a genuine treasure. Without Peters's careful research, this present volume could not have been written.

Praying Luther's Small Catechism moves sequentially through the Six Chief Parts of the Small Catechism as well as the Daily Prayers and Table of Duties. Each section begins with material from the Small Catechism followed by a prayer developed out of the catechetical material. Subsequent commentary on the doctrine of the passage reflects on how this teaching shapes our praying. The book is aimed at pastors who regularly preach and teach from the catechism, but it is also intended for laypeople, especially parents, as Luther saw the head of the household as the primary catechist for the family. There are always more treasures

---

25 FC Ep Summary 5; K-W 487.

to be discovered in the catechism, so whether the readers are veteran teachers of the Church or those who have only a passing acquaintance with Luther's little jewel, it is hoped that readers will be drawn into a deeper and lasting appreciation of this handbook for doctrine, vocation, and prayer. It is especially desired that your own praying of the catechism will be enlivened and enlarged.

While I alone bear the responsibilities for the inadequacies of this volume, many have contributed to it, perhaps without even knowing that they were doing so. I first learned the catechism from my own parents, John and Betty Pless. Pastor Eldon Roever, who baptized and confirmed me at Mount Zion Lutheran Church in Conover, North Carolina, had been a student of J. Michel Reu at Wartburg Seminary and taught me the catechism with persuasiveness and clarity. Time spent with Norman Nagel at the Chapel of the Resurrection at Valparaiso University deepened my understanding of the theology of the catechism and its use for prayer and pastoral care. Peter Bender, at that time a pastor in Boone, Iowa, attended a continuing education class on the catechism with Dr. Kenneth F. Korby at Flat-head Lake in Montana in August 1988 from which we thankfully would never recover. Pastor Bender remains a catechist without equal, and I am grateful for his friendship, fraternity in office, and his ongoing insights into the catechism. Theological conversation partners of long standing on all things Lutheran and catechetical—since 1983 when we were all living in the Twin Cities—are Robert Kolb and James Nestingen. Not to be overlooked are the students who have taken my course in catechetics both here at Concordia Theological Seminary, Fort Wayne, Indiana, and also at Lutheran Theological Seminary, Pretoria, South Africa, as well as pastors in various conferences both in the United States and abroad. Thanks are also due to Julia Hipkins, our faculty secretary, who graciously helped me with technical matters in preparing the manuscript for publication. Books are never the product of an individual but are the accumulation of learning from those who have gone before us in the faith and those who walk alongside us in this earthly pilgrimage. Thanks be to God for them all.

John T. Pless
Ascension Day 2015

CHAPTER 1

Praying the Catechism

*"A Christian without prayer is just as impossible
as a living person without a pulse."*[1]

We are accustomed to thinking in terms of studying the Small Catechism or learning it by heart, but rarely do we hear Martin Luther's language of praying the catechism.[2] The catechism functioned, for Luther, as a book of prayer. To be sure, the catechism is a handbook of Christian doctrine, laying out both the evangelical contours and biblical content of the faith, but it is more than a textbook. It is a prayer book. This can be seen from the path that Luther traveled in producing the catechism, as well as in the ways the catechism was used after its publication in 1529. Albrecht Peters captures Luther's intention:

> Praying the catechism is not merely for children and the simple; it is no less the duty and the joy of the mature Christian. Because the triune God Himself is the true teacher of the basic mysteries of the faith, all Christians are His pupils. Prayerful meditation on those central texts of our Christian faith draws our inner man into the dynamic of the Spirit of God. These texts and the light of faith breaking forth from them pull us out of evil thoughts, still the diffuse

---

1 Luther, cited by Albrecht Peters, *Lord's Prayer*, trans. Daniel Thies, Commentary on Luther's Catechisms 3 (St. Louis: Concordia, 2011), 29.

2 Kenneth F. Korby observes that "the *Small Catechism* (1529), intended to be prayed, made a lasting impression on evangelical prayer. In that catechism, in addition to prayer instruction by means of the exposition of the Ten Commandments, the Creed, and the Our Father . . . Luther gave simple instructions for family prayer that became a kind of 'house' " ("Prayer: Pre-Reformation to the Present," in *Christians at Prayer*, ed. John Gallen, S.J. [Notre Dame, IN: University of Notre Dame Press, 1977], 123).

unrest of our hearts, and form a sturdy protective barrier against demonic temptations.[3]

Prayer learns how to listen to the Word of the Lord and out of that listening to speak to Him. In so doing, prayer is the Christian's engagement in battle against Satan. There is no neutrality here; either one is aligned with the triune God or with the devil.

Such praying is serious business; it is not mindless meditation or wordless impulses to connect with a higher spiritual power. Prayer learns how to listen to the Word of the Lord and out of that listening to speak to Him. In so doing, prayer is the Christian's engagement in battle against Satan. There is no neutrality here; either one is aligned with the triune God or with the devil.[4]

Positively, to pray the catechism is to learn how to speak to God the Father in the name of the Son through the Holy Spirit who calls us to faith in the Gospel. It is based on God's command and promise. Negatively, this same prayer is directed against the devil as he would pull us away from the Father through distrust of the Son, causing us to doubt the promises of the Gospel. For Luther, prayer involves spiritual warfare, and the catechism is weaponry for this battle, both defensively and offensively.

The power of the catechism is the power of the Word of God which, it carries. Peters continues:

> Thus, for the reformer, the catechism, this instruction for children, this "laymen's bible," "does not only stand at the beginning of the way into Scripture but also at its end. It does not only function as an opening key but also as a gathering repository." Day by day Luther has placed all his theological insights and spiritual experiences into the earthen vessels of these simple formulae. These simple words "in which the Word of God became nourishing food and protecting shelter for generations" are not too difficult for the young pupil, yet they contain abyssal mysteries into which the mature Christian sinks. The catechism is accessible

For Luther, prayer involves spiritual warfare, and the catechism is weaponry for this battle, both defensively and offensively.

---

3   Albrecht Peters, *Ten Commandments*, trans. Holger Sonntag, Commentary on Luther's Catechisms 1 (St. Louis: Concordia, 2009), 33.

4   Note the observation of Peters: "Studying and praying the catechism takes place on the battlefield between God and anti-god; there is no neutrality here. Nobody stands for himself here" (Peters, *Ten Commandments*, 31).

to the beginner learning the ABCs and goes infinitely beyond the insight of the wisest. This property it shares with God's revelation.[5]

As early as July 1516, Luther preached on the catechism. By 1522, the practice had been established in Wittenberg of preaching on the catechism four times each year. The catechism sermons Luther preached from November 30 to December 18, 1528, are laden with vocabulary he will use just weeks later in the Small Catechism.[6] Luther's catechisms (both the Small and the Large) were born in the pulpit. Heinrich Bornkamm describes the birth:

> The Large Catechism is one of Luther's greatest artistic achievements. From this initial work a second sprang forth, The Small Catechism. While the mastery of the larger work lies in the wealth and liveliness of its articulating the faith, the beauty of the smaller work lies in the precision with which it made matters of faith luminous and memorable. Without the preparatory condensation of the catechetical sermons into The Large Catechism, there would have been no crystallization of the entire substance into The Small Catechism.[7]

Not only were the catechisms derived from preaching, they would serve the hearers in providing a hermeneutical framework to understand the sermon and thus help them respond to God's Word in prayer.

---

5   Peters, *Ten Commandments*, 35 (none of the quotations in this passage could be located definitively in Luther's writings). More than ten years after preparing the Small Catechism, Luther expresses the importance of the catechism and prayer in *On the Councils and the Church*, where he delineates seven marks of the Church: "Sixth, the holy Christian people are externally recognized by prayer, public praise, and thanksgiving to God. Where you see and hear the Lord's Prayer prayed and taught; or psalms or other spiritual songs sung, in accordance with the word of God and the true faith; also the creed, the Ten Commandments, and the catechism used in public, you may rest assured that a holy Christian people of God are present" (AE 41:164).

6   See *Ten Sermons on the Catechism*, AE 51:135–93.

7   Heinrich Bornkamm, *Luther in Mid-Career, 1521–1530*, ed. Karin Bornkamm, trans. E. Theodore Bachmann (Philadelphia: Fortress, 1983), 601. Also note Reinhard Slenczka: "The catechisms of Luther emerged from a series of sermons, and this might serve as a reminder that they are actual proclamation and catechization. They are, therefore, not to be put back on the shelf like a common book. In the preface to the Small Catechism we find two observations that are foundational for pastoral care. On the one hand, Luther states that every member of the congregation—not only the children—needs to know this basic knowledge of the Christian faith, that is, needs to memorize it. Having memorized the text, then they can begin to integrate and apply it to their life. Luther's thrust is that the language of the faith must be learned first and must be memorized. To use more than one form will confuse things" ("Luther's Care of Souls for Our Times," *Concordia Theological Quarterly* 67, no. 1 [January 2003]: 42).

Luther provided documents designed to replace the "confessional manuals" of the Medieval Church. Included in this category were short tracts on the Ten Commandments, Creed, Lord's Prayer, and especially on penance. Composed for laypeople, these tracts were aimed at assisting evangelical Christians in making a salutary confession of their sins in repentance wrought by the Law and then in laying hold of the forgiveness of sins delivered in the words of the absolution. These early pastoral texts would be building blocks as Luther moved to provide a concise form of Christian teaching geared toward repentance, faith, and holy living.

The appearance of the *Personal Prayer Book* in 1522 certainly was one of the building blocks Luther would use in the construction of the Small Catechism; in fact, William Russell calls it a "proto-catechism."[8] In this attempt to build an evangelical piety among those who adhered to the Reformation, Luther was offering a catechetical alternative to the popular "personal prayer books," which he considered to be laden with "un-Christian tomfoolery about prayers to God and his saints."[9] Instead, Luther stated his intent "to offer this simple Christian form of prayer and mirror for recognizing sin, based on the Lord's Prayer and the Ten Commandments."[10]

The Decalogue, the Creed, and the Lord's Prayer became the backbone of Luther's *Personal Prayer Book.* Luther gives examples of how each commandment is broken and kept. Each article of the Apostles' Creed is explained in a concise narrative. The individual petitions of the Lord's Prayer become the basis for prayers that Luther constructs to unpack their meaning. The language as well as conceptual themes used by Luther in the *Personal Prayer Book* will resurface seven years later in both the Small and Large Catechisms.

One should not overlook Luther's hymns as a source for the language and imagery that would be expressed in the Small Catechism. In 1523–24, Luther would write several hymns, including hymns on the Ten Commandments ("These Are the Holy Ten Commands," *LSB* 581), the Apostles' Creed ("We All Believe in One True God," *LSB* 954), Confession ("From Depths of Woe I Cry to Thee," *LSB* 607), and the Lord's Supper ("Jesus Christ, Our Blessed Savior," *LSB* 627). Four of Luther's "catechism hymns" predate the appearance of the Small Catechism itself. Only the hymns on the Lord's Prayer ("Our Father, Who from Heaven Above," *LSB* 766) and Baptism ("To Jordan Came the Christ, Our Lord," *LSB*

---

8   William Russell, *Praying for Reform: Martin Luther, Prayer, and the Christian Life* (Minneapolis: Augsburg Fortress, 2005), 25.

9   *Personal Prayer Book* (1522), AE 43:11.

10   *Personal Prayer Book* (1522), AE 43:12.

406) come after the publication of the Small Catechism. It is significant that in the four catechism hymns that predate the Small Catechism, Luther is using these core catechetical texts to tutor Christians in prayer using words and phrases that will be crafted into the explanations included in the Small Catechism a few years later.[11]

The Small Catechism was born amid the pressures of the 1520s. After Luther's excommunication in 1520 and the Diet of Worms in 1521, Luther would be faced with a series of critical events, including the debate with Erasmus on the enslavement of the will in 1524–26, the eruption of the Peasants' War in 1524, and ongoing doctrinal struggles against his Roman opponents and various sectarians who thought that his reforms were incomplete at best and heretical at worst. Luther had long recognized the need to bring the evangelical faith into the daily lives of ordinary people, as can be seen from his pastoral tracts and his liturgical reforms. In the preface to his German Mass of 1526, he contends that this liturgy "needs a plain and simple, fair and square catechism."[12] Here the reformer argues that such a catechism is necessary so that "the heathen who want to be Christians are taught and guided in what they should believe, know, do, and leave undone, according to the Christian faith."[13] Luther then provides some examples as to how this catechization might function and what it might look like in a question-and-answer format. Luther recognized that such catechization would be a necessary compass for the liturgical service as it oriented worshipers to faith in God's promise and love for the neighbor.

> *Luther had long recognized the need to bring the evangelical faith into the daily lives of ordinary people.*

The 1526 order of service would also include catechetical components such as the paraphrase of the Lord's Prayer and the exhortation to communicants prior

---

11   For an extensive and rich treatment of these hymns, see Robin Leaver, *Luther's Liturgical Music: Principles and Implications* (Grand Rapids: Eerdmans, 2007). On the use of these catechism hymns as a means of transmission of Christian doctrine, see Christopher Boyd Brown, *Singing the Gospel: Lutheran Hymns and the Success of the Reformation* (Cambridge, MA: Harvard University Press, 2005), 9–11, 91–94, and Christopher Boyd Brown, "Devotional Life in Hymns, Liturgy, Music, and Prayer," in *Lutheran Ecclesiastical Culture, 1550–1675*, ed. Robert Kolb (Leiden: Brill, 2008), 205–58. In this later piece, Brown notes: "One of the most prominent manifestations of Lutheran confidence in the hymns as vehicles for the Word of God was the development and use of a cycle of hymns based on the parts of the Catechism. Beginning with the 1529 Wittenberg hymnal, nearly all Lutheran hymnals for general use identified a section as *Katechismuslieder*. In the Large Catechism Luther recommended that pastors teach these hymns to the children as soon as they had learned the basic texts of the Commandments, Creed, Lord's Prayer, and the dominical institution of the sacraments" (216).

12   *German Mass and Order of Service* (1526), AE 53:64.

13   *German Mass and Order of Service* (1526), AE 53:64.

to the consecration. In the paraphrase of the Lord's Prayer, Luther catechizes the congregation in how to pray by unpacking each petition so that it might be understood and rightly prayed. Words and phrases from this liturgical paraphrase will find their way into the third chief part of the Small Catechism. Likewise, in the exhortation to communicants, Luther seeks to set the benefits of Christ's redemption before those who will come to receive Christ's body and blood so that they appropriate the Sacrament not as a sacrificial action of the priest but as the new testament of the forgiveness of sins. Again, motifs present in this liturgical admonition will work their way into the sixth chief part of the catechism.

Luther's own catechisms may be seen as a response to Pastor Nicholas Hausmann's 1524 plea that Luther prepare a catechism for use in the instruction of the "common folk." The controversy between Johann Agricola and Philip Melanchthon on the place of the Law in the Christian life accented the need for a pattern of instruction that would distinguish God's Law from His promises, repentance from faith. Ultimately it was Luther's own participation in the Saxon Visitation of 1528 that prompted him to complete the catechisms as a remedy to the maladies diagnosed in the visits.[14] The impact of the Saxon Visitation is seen in Luther's preface to the Small Catechism:

> The deplorable, wretched deprivation that I recently encountered while I was a visitor has constrained and compelled me to prepare this catechism, or Christian instruction, in such a brief, plain, and simple version. Dear God, what misery I beheld! The ordinary person, especially in the villages, knows absolutely nothing about the Christian faith, and unfortunately many pastors are completely unskilled and incompetent teachers. Yet supposedly they all bear the name Christian, are baptized, and receive the holy sacrament, even though they do not know the Lord's Prayer, the Creed, or the Ten Commandments! As a result they live like simple cattle or irrational pigs and, despite the fact that the gospel has returned, have mastered the fine art of misusing all their freedom.[15]

---

14   For more on the Saxon Visitation and its relationship to the formation of the catechisms, see "The Visitation and the Catechisms: Diagnosis and Remedy," in John T. Pless, *Martin Luther: Preacher of the Cross—A Study of Luther's Pastoral Theology* (St. Louis: Concordia, 2013), 29–41.

15   SC Preface 1–3; K-W 347–48.

Recognizing the severity of the conditions of these early Lutheran congregations, Luther believed that a pattern of catechetical instruction for both preachers and hearers of God's Word was a necessity.

Luther saw the catechism as a book to be used in home and congregation. According to Charles Arand, "while Luther addressed the catechisms to pastors, he still envisioned the head of the household as the primary teacher."[16] James Nestingen observes: "The *Small Catechism,* in chart and pamphlet form, quickly became one of the most important documents of the Lutheran Reformation. It moved the village altar into the family kitchen, literally bringing instruction in the faith home to the intimacies of family life."[17] The careful literary craftsmanship evidenced in Luther's nuanced phrases and his repetition of key words would make the catechism a useful tool for reinforcing the evangelical message that the laity were hearing from Saxon pulpits as God's Word echoed in ordinary households.

The catechism provided a basic summary of Christian doctrine along with a template for teaching. Luther's pattern for catechesis is outlined in the Preface to the Small Catechism: (a) Avoid changes or variations in the text. (b) After people have learned the text, teach them to understand it. (c) Once people have been taught the shorter catechism, take up the longer catechism.[18] Here Luther demonstrated the way in which the catechism could be learned as the pattern of sound words and stable foundation for the Christian's existence.

Luther intended the Small Catechism to be a handbook for Christian doctrine, a prayer book, and a book for the ongoing Christian life. The theological structure of the Small Catechism is geared to the proper distinction of Law and Gospel. Luther departs from the traditional, medieval ordering of the chief parts as Lord's Prayer, Creed, and Ten Commandments. He explains his rationale for the sequencing of the Decalogue, Creed, and Our Father:

> Thus the commandments teach man to recognize his sickness, enabling him to perceive what he must do or refrain from doing, consent to or refuse, and so he will recognize himself a sinful and wicked person. The Creed will teach and show him where to find the medicine—grace—which will help him to become devout and keep the commandments. The Creed points him to God and his mercy, given and made plain to him in Christ. Finally, the Lord's

---

16   Charles Arand, *That I May Be His Own: An Overview of Luther's Catechisms* (St. Louis: Concordia, 2000), 95.

17   James A. Nestingen, *Martin Luther: A Life* (Minneapolis: Augsburg, 2003), 76.

18   SC Preface 7–8; K-W 348–49.

Prayer teaches all this, namely, through the fulfillment of God's commandments everything will be given him. In these three are the essentials of the entire Bible.[19]

The ordering of the catechetical core as Decalogue, Apostles' Creed, and Lord's Prayer was a conscious move on Luther's part. The command (Decalogue) and the creed (promise) leads to prayer (Lord's Prayer). Herbert Girgensohn captures the significance of Luther's sequencing of the first three parts:

> Law, gospel, and prayer are the chief elements of the Christian faith according to the Scriptures. Luther calls the law and the gospel the "arguments," that is, the fundamentals necessary for an understanding of the Scriptures; they represent the real content of the Scriptures. The law and the gospel constitute the first two parts of the Catechism. Only one who knows the law and the gospel knows how to speak of God rightly, knows what God intends to say in the Scriptures. Then comes prayer as the third part. Prayer is the expression of the new situation and attitude of man in the presence of God, the attitude of the man who has allowed the law and the gospel to be addressed to him and accepted them in faith.[20]

God addresses human beings in Law and Gospel, working repentance and faith. In prayer, believers now address God, calling Him "Father" and imploring Him for all that He has promised. According to Peters, Luther "sets this intensive praying of the catechism against the despising of God's Word."[21]

Peters describes four dimensions of the Small Catechism for Christian teaching, praying, and living:

> (1) The catechism, as "a brief summary and digest" of the Bible, strives to comprehend its central content. It desires to summarize and lay out in simple terms the statements of the biblical witness of the revelation of God the Father through Jesus Christ, the Son, in the Holy Spirit that are decisive for salvation. (2) The catechism enunciates the spiritual core of Scripture not as an insight gained by a spiritually gifted individual, but by means of those texts that

---

19 *Personal Prayer Book* (1522), AE 43:4.

20 Herbert Girgensohn, *Teaching Luther's Catechism*, trans. John W. Doberstein (Philadelphia: Muhlenberg Press, 1959), 1:4.

21 Peters, *Ten Commandments*, 25.

have prevailed in Christendom and, at the same time, within the context of the history of interpretation of these decisive texts. This is how the reformer circumspectly makes his confession a part of the witness of the Western Church. . . . (3) The catechism looks at the concrete daily life of the simple members of the Church. It takes our calling and estate into consideration and understands both as the place in life God gave us in the coordinate system of natural/creaturely, societal/social, as well as historical/cultural, relations. In our daily life, we Christians should exercise and prove faith in love. The catechism desires to instruct for this purpose, not only as a doctrinal, confessional book but also as a book of prayer and comfort. (4) The catechism moves Scripture, the confession of the Church, and our daily life into the light of the Last Day. [The catechism should be viewed in light of] the beginning of Luther's 1522 Invocavit Sermons . . . : "The summons of death comes to us all, and no one can die for another. Everyone must fight his own battle with death by himself, alone. . . . Therefore, every one for himself must know and be armed with the chief things that concern a Christian."[22]

The catechism contained the essential elements of the Christian faith. "For Luther, knowledge of the catechism is a mark of the Christian."[23]

By teaching the faith, the catechism also teaches us how to pray.

By teaching the faith, the catechism also teaches us how to pray. Not only does the catechism teach us how to pray, but it can be prayed. Luther demonstrated how the catechism is to be prayed in his celebrated 1535 letter, *A Simple Way to Pray*, addressed to Peter Beskendorf, the town barber in Wittenberg. Here Luther uses catechesis for the life of prayer, demonstrating that there is both discipline and freedom in the praying of the catechism.[24] Rather than

---

22   Peters, *Ten Commandments*, 20. This can be seen in one of Luther's final letters to his wife, written on February 7, 1546, in which he consoles her amid her worries and anxiety: "Dear Katie: You should read the Gospel according to Saint John and the Small Catechism, of which you once said, 'Everything in this book has to do with me!' You are worrying in God's stead as if he were not almighty" (*Luther: Letters of Spiritual Counsel*, trans. and ed. Theodore G. Tappert [Philadelphia: Westminster, 1955], 105–6).

23   Gerhard Bode, "Instruction of the Christian Faith by Lutherans after Luther," in *Lutheran Ecclesiastical Culture 1550–1675*, ed. Robert Kolb (Leiden: Brill, 2008), 164.

24   Note the observation of Martin Brecht: "Nowhere is the connection between order and freedom in Luther's practice of prayer so clearly demonstrated as in his advice for Master Peter" (*Martin Luther: The Preservation of the Church 1532–1546*, trans. James L. Schaaf [Minneapolis: Fortress Press, 1993], 14).

constraining and confining, the texts of the catechism serve to anchor the praying Christian in God's Word as the "breathing space of the Holy Spirit," to borrow language from Oswald Bayer, so that the believer is ushered into the expansive vistas of God's mercy and grace in Christ. Here the Christian is freed to confess and praise, to be taught by God and guided with His truth.[25]

Before coming to the catechetical texts, Luther provides Peter with some preliminary instruction on prayer. Recognizing that both the flesh and the devil incessantly attempt to derail the practice of prayer, Luther counsels the barber out of his own experience: "When I feel that I have become cool and joyless in prayer because of other tasks and thoughts (for the flesh and the devil always impede or obstruct prayer), I take my little psalter, hurry to my room, or, if it be the day and hour for it, to the church where a congregation is assembled and, as time permits, I say quietly to myself and word-for-word the Ten Commandments, the Creed, and, if I have time, some words of Christ or of Paul, or some psalms, just as a child might do."[26] Luther sees this verbal meditation as kindling the heart for prayer.

A daily routine of prayer is recommended to Peter as a salutary discipline: "It is a good thing to let prayer be the first business of the morning and the last at night."[27] Establishing set times for prayer does not contradict the biblical dictum to pray without ceasing (Luke 11:9–13; 1 Thessalonians 5:17; Psalm 1:1). Nor does the practice segregate prayer from daily life, as Luther asserts that prayer and work go hand in hand. For faith, work is prayer. For unbelief, work becomes the opposite of prayer, that is, it becomes cursing.

The evil one tempts us not to pray:

> Yet we must be careful not to break the habit of true prayer and imagine other works to be necessary which, after all, are nothing of the kind. Thus at the end we become lax and lazy, cool and listless toward prayer. The devil who besets us is not lazy or careless, and

---

25   M. E. Schild notes: "The instructions to Master Peter reveal the great catechetismal texts of Scripture and the Church as the basis of Luther's spirituality. They are basic for him, not simply because of the value set upon them by church tradition, but because they embody the very words and promises to which God stands committed. Already in 1519 in a sermon, *On Rogationtide Prayer and Procession*, Luther stresses the two-edged point that Christian prayer is not self-help; on the contrary, it requires, results from, relies upon, and appeals to the divine promise which precedes it; it builds upon the faithfulness of a God who has promised to hear us, and is a direct expression of his trustworthiness" ("Praying the Catechism and Defrocking the Devil: Aspects of Luther's Spirituality," *Lutheran Theological Journal* 10, no. 2 [August 1976]: 49).

26   *Simple Way to Pray* (1535), AE 43:193.

27   *Simple Way to Pray* (1535), AE 43:193.

our flesh is too ready and eager to sin and is disinclined to the spirit of prayer.[28]

Therefore, Luther sees it necessary to help Peter and other Christians learn how to pray according to God's command and promise.

Luther gives a "model prayer" that serves as a preface to the Lord's Prayer. This prayer includes a confession of unworthiness on account of sin. It then moves to ground the prayer in the command and promise of God, echoing the language of the Small Catechism even as it implores the Father in the name of Jesus and in communion with "all thy saints and Christians on earth."[29]

Each petition is used as a foundation and platform for praying. Luther shows Peter how to unpack each petition for supplication and intercession while providing model prayers as well as pastoral instruction along the way. For example, see under the Fifth Petition Luther's parenthetical admonition concerning the person unable to forgive his neighbor.[30]

Faith is essential for prayer. The great word of prayer is "Amen." It is the word of faith that binds us together with all Christians:

> Finally, mark this, that you must always speak the Amen firmly. Never doubt that God in his mercy will surely hear you and say "yes" to your prayers. Never think that you are kneeling or standing alone, rather think that the whole of Christendom, all devout Christians, are standing there beside you and you are standing among them in a common, united petition which God cannot disdain. Do not leave your prayer without having said or thought, "Very well, God has heard my prayer; this I know as a certainty and a truth." That is what Amen means.[31]

Praying the Lord's Prayer does not bind us to "words or syllables" but focuses attention on the thoughts comprehended therein.

> It may happen occasionally that I may get lost among so many ideas in one petition that I forgo the other six. If such an abundance of good thoughts comes to us we ought to disregard the other petitions, make room for such thoughts, listen in silence, and under

---

28   *Simple Way to Pray* (1535), AE 43:194.

29   *Simple Way to Pray* (1535), AE 43:194–95.

30   See *Simple Way to Pray* (1535), AE 43:197.

31   *Simple Way to Pray* (1535), AE 43:198.

no circumstances obstruct them. The Holy Spirit himself preaches here, and one word of his sermon is far better than a thousand of our prayers. Many times I have learned more from one prayer than I might have learned from much reading and speculation.[32]

For Luther, there is no need to rush through the Lord's Prayer. One can be drawn into the depth of its richness as it encompasses all things for which the Christian is authorized to pray.

There is no need to rush through the Lord's Prayer. That the Lord's Prayer may be prayed at such a leisurely pace does not mean that it is prayed mindlessly. Just as a barber has to pay attention to how he uses his razor, so must the Christian attend to his prayers with "concentration and singleness of heart."[33] Therefore Luther concludes:

> This in short is the way I use the Lord's Prayer when I pray it. To this day I suckle at the Lord's Prayer like a child, and as an old man eat and drink from it and never get my fill. It is the very best prayer, even better than the psalter, which is so very dear to me. It is surely evident that a real master composed and taught it. What a great pity that the prayer of such a master is prattled and chattered so irreverently all over the world! . . . In a word, the Lord's Prayer is the greatest martyr on earth (as are the name and word of God). Everybody tortures and abuses it; few take comfort and joy in its proper use.[34]

Along with the Lord's Prayer, Luther teaches Peter how to pray the Decalogue, offering a fourfold template for praying the Ten Commandments:

> I take one part after another and free myself as much as possible from distractions in order to pray. I divide each commandment into four parts, thereby fashioning a garland of four strands. That is, I think of each commandment as, first, instruction, which is really what it is intended to be, and consider what the Lord God demands of me so earnestly. Second, I turn it into a thanksgiving; third, a confession, and fourth, a prayer.[35]

---

32 *Simple Way to Pray* (1535), AE 43:198.
33 *Simple Way to Pray* (1535), AE 43:199.
34 *Simple Way to Pray* (1535), AE 43:200.
35 *Simple Way to Pray* (1535), AE 43:200.

Luther then provides model prayers. For example, with the First Commandment, Luther sees these four parts: (1) Instruction—God teaches and expects us to have faith in no one or nothing other than God Himself. (2) Thanksgiving—God is our God. He has provided us with all that we are and all that we have. (3) Confession—we acknowledge our "countless acts of idolatry" and our ingratitude. (4) Prayer—we petition God to preserve us from unbelief and ingratitude.[36] According to this pattern of instruction, thanksgiving, confession, and prayer, Luther says we see the Ten Commandments "in their fourfold aspect, namely, as a school text, song book, penitential book, and prayer book."[37]

The Apostles' Creed is also suggested as a text to kindle prayer using the same template: "If you have more time, or the inclination, you may treat the Creed in the same manner and make it into a garland of four strands."[38] Luther then shows how this is to be done with each article of the Creed.

When it comes to prayer, sometimes less is more. Peter is cautioned to beware of attempting too much: "Take care, however, not to undertake all of this or so much that one becomes weary in spirit."[39] Luther did not want to overburden the laity with ponderous exercises that would discourage perseverance and singleness of heart in prayer. The texts of the catechism offer both depth and simplicity, providing the Christian with space for reflection and meditation.

Luther's reformatory work prior to the publication of the Small Catechism in 1529 was reshaping not only a deformed doctrine but malpractices in Christian praying. As we see from his tract for Peter the barber, the catechism would become not only a primer for prayer but a text that could be prayed. Thus more than three centuries later, Wilhelm Löhe would conclude that "no catechism in the world but this can be prayed."[40] The words of a late Reformation hymn become our prayer as well:

> **Lord, help us ever to retain**
> **The Catechism's doctrine plain**
> **As Luther taught the Word of truth**
> **In simple style to tender youth.** (*LSB* 865:1)

---

36   *Simple Way to Pray* (1535), AE 43:200–201.

37   *Simple Way to Pray* (1535), AE 43:209.

38   *Simple Way to Pray* (1535), AE 43:209.

39   *Simple Way to Pray* (1535), AE 43:209.

40   Wilhelm Löhe, *Three Books about the Church*, trans. and ed. James L. Schaaf (Philadelphia: Fortress, 1969), 171.

CHAPTER 2

The Ten Commandments

An Agenda for Christian Prayer

Luther placed the Ten Commandments at the beginning of the Small Catechism even as the Law precedes the Gospel. In the First Commandment, God asserts Himself: "You shall have no other gods" (Exodus 20:3). The reformer begins not with the prologue from Exodus 20:1—"I am the Lord your God, who brought you out of the land of Egypt, out of the house of bondage"—but with the bare fact of God's lordship. Thus in his 1525 treatise *How Christians Should Regard Moses*, Luther writes:

> This text makes it clear that even the Ten Commandments do not pertain to us. For God never led us out of Egypt, but only the Jews. The sectarian spirits want to saddle us with Moses and all the commandments. We will just skip that. We will regard Moses as a teacher, but we will not regard him as our lawgiver—unless he agrees with both the New Testament and the natural law.[1]

Luther understands the Ten Commandments as reflecting the Law written into creation. As such it demands that man recognize himself as dependent upon and accountable to the Creator. God is the one who is to be feared, loved, and trusted above all things. "Nature also has these laws. Nature provides that we should call upon God. The Gentiles attest to this fact. For there never was a Gentile who did not call upon his idols, even though these were not the true God."[2] A person

---

1   *How Christians Should Regard Moses* (1525), AE 35:165.
2   *How Christians Should Regard Moses* (1525), AE 35:168.

will call upon whomever or whatever he has as his god. Ultimately there are no atheists, for those without faith in the true God are not without a "fabricating heart"[3] with which they will craft a god to meet their need for deity, most often in their own image and likeness.

Prayer is not a uniquely Christian phenomenon; it is found, in one way or another, in all religions. Human beings cannot escape the pressure to pray just as they cannot be without a god. The question that arises with prayer is to which god is it addressed? Is prayer simply an instinctual religious reaction to a sense of the numinous, the awe-inspiring or terror-filled mystery of the cosmos, or is it the voice of faith that speaks to the Father through the Son in the unity of the Holy Spirit?

Luther sees the Ten Commandments as forming the Christian's prayer list even as the Lord's Prayer reflects the form of the Christian's life in the world.[4] As we observed in the previous chapter, when Luther instructed his friend, Peter the barber, in the art of Christian praying, he directed him to pray the Commandments one by one.

The Wittenberg barber is taught a fourfold template for praying the Ten Commandments:

> I take one part after another and free myself as much as possible from distractions in order to pray. I divide each commandment into four parts, thereby fashioning a garland of four strands. That is, I think of each commandment as, first, instruction, which is really what it is intended to be, and consider what the Lord God demands of me so earnestly. Second, I turn it into a thanksgiving; third, a confession, and fourth, a prayer.[5]

Luther provides model prayers based on the Commandments. Then Luther continues: "These are the Ten Commandments in their fourfold aspect, namely, as a school text, song book, penitential book, and prayer book. They are intended to help the heart come to itself and grow zealous in prayer."[6] The Ten Commandments are concrete; they are the demarcation of the triune God's lordship over

---

3   Oswald Bayer, *Theology the Lutheran Way*, trans. Jeffrey Silcock and Mark Mattes (Grand Rapids: Eerdmans, 2007), 26.

4   For more on this point, see Robert Kolb, *Teaching God's Children His Teaching* (St. Louis: Concordia Seminary Press, 2012), 57–77.

5   *Simple Way to Pray* (1525), AE 43:200.

6   *Simple Way to Pray* (1525), AE 43:209.

the totality of human life. As such they delineate the spaces that are occupied by prayer day in and day out. Such prayer follows from the First Commandment.

The First Commandment
You shall have no other gods

What does this mean?
We should fear, love, and trust in God above all things.

Lord God, You require us to fear, love, and trust in You above all things. Grant unto us undivided hearts to fear Your wrath and so avoid the evil that You abhor. Instead, help us to love what You command and trust in Your promises; through Jesus Christ, Your Son, who lives and reigns with You and the Holy Spirit, one God, world without end. Amen.

In the Large Catechism, Luther defines what it means to have a god:

> A "god" is the term for that to which we are to look for all good and in which we are to find refuge in all need. Therefore, to have a god is nothing else than to trust and believe in that one with your whole heart. As I have often said, it is the trust and faith of the heart alone that make both God and an idol. If your faith and trust are right, then your God is the true one. Conversely, where your trust is false and wrong, there you do not have the true God. For these belong together, faith and God. Anything on which your heart relies and depends, I say, that is really your God.[7]

Counterfeit gods are the idols that the heart makes to establish itself and provide security. So Luther continues:

> There are some who think that they have God and everything they need when they have money and property . . . on which they set their whole heart. . . . Thus you can easily understand what and

---

7   LC I 2–3; K-W 386.

how much this commandment requires, namely, that one's whole heart and confidence be placed in God alone, and in no one else.[8]

If one does not have the true God—that is, the God and Father of our Lord Jesus Christ—he or she will take recourse in the idolatry of self-made deities or, like the fool in Psalm 14, protest that there is no God. Gerhard Forde rightly observes: "Cut off from God, conscience drives us ultimately to wish there were no God. Apart from Christ, atheism is finally the only hope."[9] The assertion is necessitated by the human being's inability to will that God be God, which would mean that the individual is dethroned of his perceived lordship over life.

To use the words of Albrecht Peters:

> God's First Commandment, however, confiscates this center of our entire human nature for itself. God, as our Creator, calls our heart out of clinging to what is created and demands it for itself in an exclusive and undivided way. Here the First Commandment and the Creed interlock.[10]

It is only this confiscated heart—fearing, loving, and trusting in God above all things—that is free to pray in the fashion that God commands and promises to hear. Such prayer is not easy; it involves struggle, for "when we meditate on the first commandment we are involved in a battle between the one Lord and the

---

8   LC I 5, 13; K-W 387–88. Without faith, the prodigal heart has only unbelief and cannot seek God or call upon Him. Hans Joachim Iwand says: "Unbelief . . . is to seek one's own justice; to defend it over against God's justice; to insist on one's own achievements; to measure everything—both what is earthly and one's own life before God—by one's own concept of good and evil. It means to measure God himself by what we consider just and unjust, possible and impossible, useful and harmful, good and bad. Unbelief is the only sin against the First Commandment, which is the source and principle of all other transgressions" (*The Righteousness of Faith According to Luther,* ed. Virgil F. Thompson, trans. Randi H. Lundell [Eugene, OR: Wipf & Stock, 2008], 23); used by permission of Wipf & Stock Publishers. www.wipfandstock.com.

9   Gerhard Forde, "Justification," in *Christian Dogmatics,* ed. Carl Braaten and Robert Jenson (Philadelphia: Fortress, 1984), 2:418. Also: "The primal temptation of man is rebellion against the First Commandment, and once that rebellion takes place it enslaves men to the countless powers which are not God" (Girgensohn, *Teaching Luther's Catechism,* 1:33).

10   Albrecht Peters, *Ten Commandments,* 118. Also see John A. Maxfield: "For Luther idolatry is the self-enslaving false worship of a heart turned in on itself, of religious piety shaped by self-will and thus works righteousness in any number of ways, of substituting human reason for the revelation of God in the divine Word" ("Martin Luther and Idolatry," in *The Reformation as Christianization: Essays on Scott Hendrix's Christianization Thesis,* ed. Anna Marie Johnson and John A. Maxfield [Tübingen: Mohr Siebeck, 2012], 168).

many lords (cf. 1 Cor. 8:5f.)."[11] To pray from the First Commandment is to let God be God, and for the flesh, the world, and the devil, that is a declaration of war.

The First Commandment is foundational for prayer. It demands an undivided heart, that is, a heart that clings to God alone. Oswald Bayer has observed that the First Commandment functions as both Law and Gospel.[12] It is Law in that it absolutely prohibits every rival deity. But hidden under the prohibition is the good news that to have Jesus Christ as Lord means that you need no other god. Prayer grounded in the First Commandment is not an exercise in futile idolatry, but it is calling on the only God there is, the God and Father of the Lord Jesus Christ.

> To pray from the First Commandment is to let God be God, and for the flesh, the world, and the devil, that is a declaration of war.

The Second Commandment
You shall not misuse the name of the Lord your God.

What does this mean?
We should fear and love God so that we do not curse, swear, use satanic arts, lie, or deceive by His name, but call upon it in every trouble, pray, praise, and give thanks.

Holy and merciful God, cause us to fear and love You so that we do not curse, swear, use satanic arts, lie, or deceive by Your name, but call upon it in every trouble, pray, praise, and give thanks and so glorify Your name, which alone is holy; through Jesus Christ, our Lord. Amen.

In a stunning series of sermons on the Ten Commandments preached just after World War II, the German theologian Paul Althaus said, "The right use of

---

11   Bayer, *Theology the Lutheran Way*, 62.

12   "The self-introduction, 'I am the Lord, your God,' is not valid in a way that is simply positivistic, self-evident, or unchallenged. For at the same time, along with it, in the very same breath, it is necessary for us to hear until our death: 'you shall have no other gods before me' (Exod. 20:2). This is law. The gospel, on the other hand says, 'you have no need of other gods!" (Oswald Bayer, "The Plurality of the One God and the Plurality of the Gods," *Pro Ecclesia* 25, no. 3 [Summer 2006]: 354).

God's name is best learned when one speaks not only about God but *with* God. Speech about God must be born of prayer, out of speaking with God."[13]

God prohibits every misuse of His name. God discloses His name by revelation; it is never a label that human beings devise for themselves. "God's saving activity is concentrated in God's name; indeed, God has 'deposited' His name here on earth so that we would have a place to find refuge."[14] In the Second Commandment, God fences His name against every form of manipulation and abuse: cursing, swearing, using superstition (satanic arts), lying, or deception. Peters observes:

God prohibits every misuse of His name.

> The prohibition against misusing the name uncovers the original sin of man: We refuse to honor God who discloses Himself to us in His name and Word, that is, in Jesus Christ. In view of the God who in creation and redemption showers His blessing on us, we go on our self-chosen paths and pursue our own honor. Yet we can gain and preserve true honor before God and man only by subjecting it to the cross of Christ and carrying it home to God.[15]

Old Testament theologian Walther Eichrodt writes of God giving His name to Israel so that "by revealing his Name God has, as it were, made himself over to them; he has opened to them a part of his very being and given them a means of access to himself."[16] The holiness of God's name coupled with the fact that by the divine name we have a sure way to call upon God lies underneath the catechism's teaching of the Second Commandment. God does not keep His name secret. He gives it to us to use freely in the way that He intends it to be used. His intended use excludes every unauthorized use of His name. "Man does not manipulate God, either by giving him a name of his own conceiving, or by presuming to make use of the supernatural powers of the Godhead by calling upon and using

---

13   Paul Althaus, *Thou Shalt! Sermons Based on the Ten Commandments*, trans. John W. Rilling (Springfield, OH: Chantry Music Press, 1971), 13.

14   Peters, *Ten Commandments*, 155. The temptation to use God's name superstitiously was present in ancient Israel: "It is conceivable that even in Israel people were at times liable to use Jahweh's name for sinister purposes dangerous to the community" (Gerhard von Rad, *Old Testament Theology*, trans. D. M. G Stalker [New York: Harper & Row, 1962], 1:183).

15   Peters, *Ten Commandments*, 157.

16   Walther Eichrodt, *Theology of the Old Testament*, trans. J. A. Baker (Philadelphia: Westminster Press, 1961), 1:207.

his name."[17] Standing in opposition to the right use of God's name would be all superstitious attempts at the incantation of spiritual powers through the invocation of the holy name.

To pray this commandment, then, is to repent of every misuse of God's name, recognizing the bridge between the First Commandment, which requires the heart to fear, love, and trust in God above all things, and the Second Commandment, which governs how our tongue gives expression to this requirement. In the Large Catechism, Luther accents this connection: "First the heart honors God by faith and then the lips by confession."[18] The catechism delineates both the negative prohibition and the positive obligation. We are not to curse, swear, use satanic arts, lie, or deceive by God's name. We are to call upon this name in every trouble, pray, praise, and give thanks. Luther cites Psalm 50:15 in the Large Catechism to demonstrate that such a use of God's name has God's command and promise behind it. There is the promise that those who call upon the name of the Lord will be saved (Joel 2:32). The righteous rejoice in their Lord and "give thanks to His holy name" (Psalm 97:12). This positive use of God's name is illustrated by Luther's exposition of the Lord's Prayer in the catechism and his inclusion of daily prayers as an appendix to the Six Chief Parts.

Third Commandment
Remember the Sabbath day by keeping it holy.

What does this mean?
We should fear and love God so that we do not despise preaching
and His Word, but hold it sacred and gladly hear and learn it.

By Your Word and Spirit, draw us away from our restless labor that we might find rest in You alone, merciful God. Grant that, fearing and loving You above all things, we may never despise the preaching of Your Word of Life, but hold it sacred and gladly hear and learn it; through Jesus Christ, our Lord. Amen.

---

17   Herbert Girgensohn, *Teaching Luther's Catechism*, 1:43–44.

18   LC I 70; K-W 395.

The command to keep the Sabbath belongs to the old covenant (see Colossians 2:16–17). "Therefore, according to its outward meaning, this commandment does not apply to us."[19] So Luther recast the commandment to demonstrate its applicability to Christians. The focus is no longer on a specific day for worship, but on the Word of God, which is the true "holy thing" that hallows us. Thus the day is sanctified or hallowed by Christians rightly using the Holy Word of God and exercising ourselves in it. Non-Christians can keep a holiday and enjoy rest and idleness, Luther says in the Large Catechism, but because they are not using God's Word, the day is not kept holy.[20]

The rest or ceasing from labor has its significance not simply for physical refreshment or rejuvenation but for the stopping of human work so God is given time and space to do His work. Vilmos Vajta puts it like this:

> In no sense is this worship [i.e., Divine Service of Word and Sacrament] a preparatory stage which faith could ultimately leave behind. Rather faith might be defined as a passive cult (*cultus passivus*) because in this life it will always depend on the worship by which God imparts Himself—a gift granted to the believing congregation. This is confirmed in Luther's Explanation of the Third Commandment. To him Sabbath rest means more than a pause from work. It should be an opportunity for God to do His work on man. God wants to distract man from his daily toil and so open him to God's gifts. To observe Sabbath is not a good work which man could offer to God. On the contrary it means pausing from all our works and letting God do His work in us and for us.
>
> Thus Luther's picture of the Sabbath is marked by the passivity of man and the activity of God. And it applies not only to certain holy days on the calendar, but to the Christian life in its entirety, testifying to man's existence as a creature of God who waits by faith for the life to come. Through God's activity in Christ, man is drawn into the death and resurrection of the Redeemer and is so recreated a new man in Christ. The Third Commandment lays on us no obligation

---

19   LC I 82; K-W 397.

20   Note Luther's comment: "Any conduct or work apart from God's Word is unholy in the sight of God, no matter how splendid and brilliant it may appear, or even if it is altogether covered with holy relics, as are the so-called spiritual walks of life, which do not know God's Word but seek holiness in their own works. Note, then, that the power and force of this commandment consists not in the resting but in the hallowing, so that this day may have its special holy function" (LC I 93–94; K-W 399).

for specific works of any kind (not even spiritual or cultic works) but rather directs us to the work of God. And we do not come into contact with the latter except in the Service, where Christ meets us in the means of grace.[21]

The Third Commandment builds a protective fence, as it were, around time so that there is a space to hear God's Word. Human busyness—even devotion to the necessary tasks of life—is not allowed to interfere with the one thing that is needful, the hearing of the words of Jesus, which are spirit and life.

This commandment is fulfilled where the triune God is doing His life-giving work through His Word.

> For this Word is not idle or dead, but effective and living. Even if no other benefit or need drove us to the Word, yet everyone should be motivated by the realization that through the Word the devil is cast out and put to flight, this commandment is fulfilled, and God is more pleased than by any hypocrisy, no matter how brilliant.[22]

When this commandment is fulfilled, hearts are set free and lips are open to call upon God in prayer, praise, and thanksgiving. But for this to take place, God's Word must first be heard, for faith comes only by hearing this saving message (Romans 10:17).

The Fourth Commandment
Honor your father and your mother.

What does this mean?
We should fear and love God so that we do not despise
or anger our parents and other authorities, but honor
them, serve and obey them, love and cherish them.

Heavenly Father, from whom all earthly fatherhood has its source: Look in mercy on Your children that we may never sin against You by despising or angering our parents and others whom You place in authority over us. Give us

---

21   Vilmos Vajta, *Luther on Worship*, trans. U. S. Leupold (Philadelphia: Muhlenberg, 1958), 130, 132.

22   LC I:101–2; K-W 400.

repentance where we have ignored, neglected, or provoked our parents, and enable us to honor, serve, obey, love, and cherish them as Your instruments for giving us life and blessing; through Jesus Christ, Your Son, our Lord. Amen.

The Fourth Commandment is pivotal because it is the first commandment in the Second Table, yet it is directed back to the majesty of God who orders creation in such a way that human beings are His tools and representatives.[23] In this way, the Fourth Commandment is tied to the First Commandment. "He who confronts man with his total claim in the First Commandment is facing him with the same claim in the Fourth Commandment."[24] Or, as Werner Elert puts it: "When we honor our parents as his substitutes we honor him."[25] This commandment cannot be fulfilled without faith, for without faith we would not see our parents as God's substitutes.

Honoring parents and others in authority translates into thanksgiving for the body and life God has given us and still sustains and protects through them. Such thanksgiving is the recognition that we are not self-created but dependent. "In birth God sets me down in a unique relationship of dependence upon two particular persons."[26] Where parents are treated as something other than the channels through which God has given life, this commandment calls for confession of sin against the Creator Himself. On the other hand, parents are loved and cherished when they are held before God in prayer.

As we pray the Fourth Commandment, parents are acknowledged with thanksgiving as the instruments through whom the Father has given life. Children intercede for their parents, imploring God for their welfare even as this commandment also calls us to repentance for the failure to honor them through loving service.

---

23   Also see Peters: "The Fourth Commandment occupies a key position between the two Tables. It already deals with our actions toward people, which is why it belongs to the Second Table. However, from these people it lifts up the men who, by virtue of God's ordering, are placed before and over us and sets them between us and God. On them rests the majesty of God's ordering in creation and by the Word; thereby they share in God's fatherly majesty itself" (*Ten Commandments*, 192–93).

24   Girgensohn, *Teaching Luther's Catechism*, 1:70. Also see Friedrich Mildenberger: "The First Commandment determined the basic character of the 'first table' of the law. Similarly, Luther's explanation treated the Fourth Commandment as basic to those commandments that refer to our relationship to the neighbor" (*Theology of the Lutheran Confessions*, ed. Robert C. Schultz, trans. Erwin Lueker [Philadelphia: Fortress, 1986], 145).

25   Werner Elert, *The Christian Ethos*, trans. Carl J. Schindler (Philadelphia: Fortress, 1957), 82.

26   Girgensohn, *Teaching Luther's Catechism*, 1:70.

The Fifth Commandment
You shall not murder.

What does this mean?
We should fear and love God so that we do not
hurt or harm our neighbor in his body, but help
and support him in every physical need.

God, defender of the weak and helper of the helpless, we implore You to sustain us with Your favor and to strengthen us by Your mercy that we might act with tenderness toward our neighbors, never hurting or harming them in their bodies by hateful words, destructive deeds, or neglect of their well-being. Instead, empower us to help and support them in every physical need even as You have shown mercy to us in Your crucified Son in whose name we pray. Amen.

In the Fifth Commandment, God guards and protects the life of the neighbor.

> The Lord surrounds the bodily life of our neighbor with a shield wall, lest we hurt him "in his body." The word "body" circumscribes the neighbor's "own person" in his earthbound physical existence. The phrase "in the body" marks the place where we encounter our fellow man and where we can take his life. Thus "body" serves as a placeholder for the person as well as the life.[27]

Thus there is a prohibition against doing anything that would hurt or harm the neighbor in his body as well as the positive requirement that we help and support him in every physical need. "The commandment is therefore understood as a protective wall which surrounds the earthly, physical existence of our neighbor, guarding it against everything which may harm and hinder it."[28]

Not only does God forbid murder in this commandment, but also "everything that may lead to murder. Many people, although they do not actually commit murder, nevertheless curse others and wish such frightful things on them that, if they were to come true, they would soon put an end to them. . . . God," Luther

---

27 Peters, *Ten Commandments*, 215.

28 Girgensohn, *Teaching Luther's Catechism*, 1:86.

explains, "wishes to remove the root and source that embitters our heart toward our neighbor."[29] For this reason, Luther urges his readers to use this commandment as a mirror to recognize the sinful urges of resentment, anger, and revenge. Instead of seeking an outlet for indignation, Luther calls on Christians to "be attentive to [God's] will and, with heartfelt confidence and prayer in his name, commit whatever wrong we suffer to God."[30]

In this way the Fifth Commandment will be prayed as we acknowledge our responsibility before God for the bodily life of the neighbor. Like the other commandments, the Fifth Commandment is linked to the First: God "always wants to remind us to recall the First Commandment, that he is our God; that is, that he wishes to help, comfort, and protect us, so that we may restrain our desire for revenge."[31] In place of the desire for retribution, Christians will pray and act to protect and preserve, guard and defend the neighbor's bodily life.

The Sixth Commandment
You shall not commit adultery.

What does this mean?
We should fear and love God so that we lead a sexually
pure and decent life in what we say and do, and
husband and wife love and honor each other.

Holy Father, You blessed our first parents in Paradise with the gift of marriage, and by Your Word You continue to unite men and women in this estate, which You have hallowed and blessed. Guard us from all dishonorable lust and every sexual sin that we may be pure and decent in all that we say or do. Answer the cries of those who seek a godly spouse, and uphold all married couples in faithfulness that they may honor and love each other and so glorify You; through Jesus Christ, who is the true Bridegroom to His Bride, the Church. Amen.

---

29 LC I 186–7; K-W 411.
30 LC I 187; K-W 411.
31 LC I 195; K-W 413.

God established marriage as the one-flesh union of man and woman in Eden before the fall into sin. After the fall, marriage, like the rest of God's creation, is subject to the corrupting powers of sin. With the Sixth Commandment, the Creator secures and protects marriage against adultery and every other sexual sin. In the Large Catechism, Luther calls marriage "the first of all institutions,"[32] which God has created as that walk of life in which man and woman, created differently, are joined together to be true to each other and to beget children and rear them to His glory. This commandment is grounded in God's purposes for marriage, and it curbs all that would defile God's order, forming a protective wall to this end.

Marriage is received as a gift of the Creator by those who know the truth (see 1 Timothy 4:1–5). It is not a product of evolutionary development or a mere legal arrangement subject to the changing whims of culture. It is received as the Creator's gift wherein He wills to extend the human family while providing a lasting bond of companionship between man and woman. Thus this commandment evokes thanksgiving for God's holy estate of marriage, and it enjoins us to pray that God would guard its holiness in our midst (see Hebrews 13:4).

The Seventh Commandment
You shall not steal.

What does this mean?
We should fear and love God so that we do not take
our neighbor's money or possessions, or get them
in any dishonest way, but help him to improve
and protect his possessions and income.

Father of light and Giver of every good gift, keep us from treating our neighbors' money or possessions as things that we are free to take for ourselves. Instead, give us charity of heart that we might help and assist our neighbors to improve and protect their possessions and income so they may live without want or neediness and so enjoy the blessings that You have bestowed on them; through Jesus Christ, our Lord. Amen.

---

32   LC I 207; K-W 414.

God asserts His lordship over the goods of this world so that we look to Him and not to our neighbors' wealth for our security. This commandment

> wants to disconnect us from depending on this world and its god, the powerless yet omnipotent Mammon. It wants to strike at the root of our earthbound existence—that worrying/greedy clinging to what is visible and at hand—and to focus our trust only at the otherworldly and invisible God. Christ again erects over us the First Commandment: what we sought from dead Mammon, this we are now to seek from the living God.[33]

Only the heart that fears, loves, and trusts in God above all things can be freed from captivation to property that belongs to another, a captivation which prompts us to take what is not ours to take.

Temporal property, the gifts of daily bread that God provides to sustain bodily life in the world, is guarded by the Seventh Commandment. The commandment is far-reaching, as the Large Catechism demonstrates in its scope. In this commandment God forbids every action that would deprive the neighbor of the gifts God has provided.

> Let all people know, then, that it is their duty, on pain of God's displeasure, not to harm their neighbors, to take advantage of them, or to defraud them by any faithless or underhanded business transaction. Much more than that, they are also obligated faithfully to protect their neighbors' property and to promote and further their interests, especially when they get money, wages, and provisions for doing so.[34]

Luther repeatedly makes the point in the Large Catechism that God uses the hangman to enforce this commandment in the world.

The flip side of the Seventh Commandment is vocation. The one who steals is to cease his thievery so that he will have something to give to those in need. The commandment enjoins us not only to refrain from taking the neighbor's money or property by outright theft, shoddy workmanship, or unethical dealings, but to help him improve and protect his livelihood. God has arranged the world in such a way that human beings are daily bread to one another. We both receive our

---

33   Peters, *Ten Commandments*, 271.

34   LC I 233; K-W 417.

daily bread through others and we are instruments and channels for the giving of daily bread to others. Theft interrupts this receiving and giving.

The confession of the Creed's First Article and the praying of the Fourth Petition of the Lord's Prayer reflect the place of the Seventh Commandment. We pray that God will guard and protect the neighbor's property and income. To pray the Seventh Commandment is to pray against our own idolatrous greed and envy. Intercession for the neighbor in his or her economic need is in accord with God's intention expressed in this commandment.

> *God has arranged the world in such a way that human beings are daily bread to one another.*

The Eighth Commandment
You shall not give false testimony against your neighbor.

What does this mean?
We should fear and love God so that we do not tell
lies about our neighbor, betray him, slander him, or
hurt his reputation, but defend him, speak well of
him, and explain everything in the kindest way.

God of truth, set a guard over the door of our lips, that our tongues may be purified from sinful speech and sanctified for the words that edify. Give us repentance where we have uttered falsehood, betrayed through exposing secrets, slandered with malicious gossip, or hurt our neighbor's reputation with lies or half-truths. Make us eager and ready to come to the defense of our neighbors, speak well of them, and explain their circumstances and actions in the kindest way. Hear us for the sake of Him who is truth incarnate, Your Son, our Lord Jesus Christ. Amen.

With the Eighth Commandment, God sets a guard over the mouth and requires us to keep watch over the doors of our lips (see Psalm 141:3), lest we speak falsehood against the neighbor or twist the truth in such a way as to harm his reputation.

> We are no longer a lying witness against the good reputation of
> our neighbor; we are henceforth a true advocate and defender of
> our neighbor, even where he has exposed his faults. Thus we show

ourselves to be sons of the Paraclete who holds up for us the good word of adoption in Christ against the accusation of Satan and of our own conscience.[35]

The lie is indicative of the rejection of the truth of God's lordship (see Psalm 50:19; Romans 1:25, 29–31; 1 Timothy 1:9–11) and so also strikes at the First Commandment. "Lying is more than a transgression of our tongue; in the final analysis, the 'lie' is our *no* to the self-disclosure of God in the Son and as such the core act of unbelief."[36] The commandment demands repentance for the sins of the lips (Colossians 3:9–10) and requires the speaking of the truth in love (see Ephesians 4:25). Rather than speaking about the neighbor with falsehood or slandering his reputation with malicious talk, mindless gossip, or reckless accusation, the tongue is disciplined to speak well of the neighbor *coram mundo* ("before the world") and pray for his blessing *coram Deo* ("before God").

The Ninth Commandment
You shall not covet your neighbor's house.

What does this mean?
We should fear and love God so that we do not scheme to get our neighbor's inheritance or house, or get it in a way which only appears right, but help and be of service to him in keeping it.

Gracious Giver of every good and perfect gift, restrain our rogue hearts as they too easily are drawn to covetousness, which is idolatry. Break every scheme that would attempt to obtain for ourselves the property that You have given to our neighbors, and grant unto us contentment with the daily bread You have freely and without merit granted to us; through Jesus Christ, our Lord. Amen.

With the final two commandments, we have come full circle back to the First Commandment. To covet is to commit idolatry (see Ephesians 5:5), which leads

---

35   Peters, *Ten Commandments*, 289.

36   Peters, *Ten Commandments*, 294.

to death.[37] The Ninth Commandment prohibits the idolatry that is embedded in the cunning desire to have for ourselves the property (the "inheritance or house") that God has given to the neighbor. This commandment is an intensification of the Seventh Commandment; it is directed against the sins of desire cataloged in 1 Timothy 6:6–10. This coveting is described as "the desires of the eyes and pride in possessions" in 1 John 2:16, where it also is identified as "not from the Father but is from the world." Such coveting is not merely secret desires and urgings of the errant heart, but it is made concrete in schemes and undertakings that would acquire that which belongs to another. "We shall not do justice to God's law unless we allow the commandment, 'You shall not covet,' to show us that the sinister power of desire is the hidden source of all sin within us."[38] Eve coveted God's divinity in Genesis and so was led into unbelief (Genesis 3:1–7).

The commandment obligates us to be of service to our neighbors to the end that they keep their property. Here we pray that God would lead us to recognize His generosity in giving us all that we need to support this body and life. Then with grateful hearts we can pray for our neighbors' well-being and do everything within our power to help them preserve it and prosper in this life.

The Tenth Commandment
You shall not covet your neighbor's wife, or his
manservant or maidservant, his ox or donkey, or
anything that belongs to your neighbor.

What does this mean?
We should fear and love God so that we do not entice or
force away our neighbor's wife, workers, or animals, or turn
them against him, but urge them to stay and do their duty.

Almighty God, Lord of all that is good and pure: Set our hearts on You alone so that we may not entice or force away the spouse, workers, or animals

---

37 The outcome of idolatry is death: "As our Creator and Redeemer, God does not want us to get bogged down in this perishing world of death and idolize what is perishing" (Peters, *Ten Commandments*, 310).

38 Girgensohn, *Teaching Luther's Catechism*, 1:118.

of our neighbor but urge them to fulfill their duties in the places where You have put them; through Jesus Christ, our Lord. Amen.

⸺◦◦⸺

David coveted Uriah's wife (see 2 Samuel 11), and the end result was adultery and murder. Coveting our neighbor's wife is the adultery of the heart condemned by Jesus in Matthew 5:27–28. Luring away our neighbor's spouse, workers, or livestock is yet another enactment of fleshly entitlement that seeks to assert self over God in egoistic restlessness. Thus "the prohibition becomes the anthropological counterpart of the First Commandment."[39] The opposite of covetousness is contentment (see Hebrews 13:5), which comes from the fear, love, and trust in God above all things. Only a heart set free by faith is capable of living in contentment.

⸺◦◦⸺

THE CLOSE OF THE COMMANDMENTS

What does God say about all these commandments?
He says, "I, the Lord your God, am a jealous God,
punishing the children for the sin of the fathers to the
third and fourth generation of those who hate Me, but
showing love to a thousand generations of those who love
Me and keep My commandments." (Exodus 20:5–6)

What does this mean?
God threatens to punish all who break these commandments.
Therefore, we should fear His wrath and not do anything against
them. But He promises grace and every blessing to all who
keep these commandments. Therefore, we should also love
and trust in Him and gladly do what He commands.

⸺◦◦⸺

Lord God, in Your holy jealousy You will not share us with any false gods. Unite our hearts to fear Your wrath and never disobey Your Commandments and so incur Your deserved punishment. Enable us to love and trust in You above all things that by Your grace we might receive the blessings You promise

---

39   Peters, *Ten Commandments*, 313.

to those who keep Your Commandments; through Jesus Christ, Your Son, our Lord, who lives and reigns with You and the Holy Spirit, one God, now and forever. Amen.

The relationship between the First Commandment and the remaining nine commandments is demonstrated in the Close of the Commandments in the Small Catechism. Luther demonstrated this by placing the epilogue to the First Commandment (see Exodus 20:5–6; Deuteronomy 5:9b–10) as the conclusion to the Decalogue itself. Each of the commandments is taught in light of the First Commandment.

> Thus the First Commandment is to illuminate and impart its splendor to all the others. In order that this may be constantly repeated and never forgotten, therefore, you must let these concluding words run through all the commandments, like the clasp or hoop of a wreath that binds the end to the beginning and holds everything together.[40]

God threatens punishment to those who will not fear, love, and trust in Him above all things, but He promises grace and every blessing to those who cling to Him by faith in His Son. It is only through faith that the Commandments are fulfilled and believers are enabled to call upon the name of the Lord in prayer, praise, and thanksgiving. Where God is feared, loved, and trusted above all things, lips are unsealed and tongues are loosed for prayer, which the Father delights to hear and answer.

---

40   LC I 326; K-W 430.

CHAPTER 3

The Apostles' Creed

The Trinitarian Shape of Christian Prayer

Luther recognized the ancient priority of what we have come to know as the Apostles' Creed: "The first symbol, that of the apostles, is truly the finest of all. Briefly, correctly, and in a splendid way it summarizes the articles of faith, and it can easily be learned by children and simple people."[1] Because it was the briefest and most ecumenical confession of Christendom—and it was used in the primitive church for baptismal catechesis—it was natural for Luther to use this creed for the instruction of the baptized in the trinitarian faith.[2] As Hermann Sasse reminds us, the Creed is like all Christian confession: a response to revelation telling us "objectively of facts, not of subjective experiences."[3]

The Apostles' Creed is an unpacking of Peter's confession at Caesarea Philippi that Jesus is "the Christ, the Son of the living God" (Matthew 16:16). It is the summary of "the faith that was once for all delivered to the saints" (Jude 3). The Creed "is the summation of the Gospel; when it is confessed, the triune God Himself places the description of His saving acts in one's mouth, so that we can confess faith in Him thereby and can find refuge for our faith in those words

---

1   *The Three Symbols* (1538), AE 34:201.

2   For a concise history of the Apostles' Creed, see Charles P. Arand, Robert Kolb, and James A. Nestingen, *The Lutheran Confessions: History and Theology of The Book of Concord* (Minneapolis: Fortress, 2012), 16–25.

3   Hermann Sasse, "Jesus Christ Is Lord: The Church's Original Confession," in *We Confess: Jesus Christ*, trans. Norman E. Nagel (St. Louis: Concordia, 1984), 10.

when it is under attack."[4] The Creed sets forth who it is to whom we pray. Prayer itself then becomes a confession that Jesus Christ is Lord.

Luther sets the Creed in contrast to the Decalogue as the Commandments set out God's demands and the Creed is an exposition of God's work of giving:

> From this you see that the Creed is a very different teaching than the Ten Commandments. For the latter teach us what we ought to do, but the Creed tells us what God has done for us and gives to us. The Ten Commandments, moreover, are written in the hearts of all people, but no human wisdom is able to comprehend the Creed; it must be taught by the Holy Spirit alone. Therefore the Ten Commandments do not succeed in making us Christians, for God's wrath and displeasure still remain upon us because we cannot fulfill what God demands of us. But the Creed brings pure grace and makes us righteous and acceptable to God. Through this knowledge we come to love and delight in all the commandments of God because we see here in the Creed how God gives himself completely to us, with all his gifts and power, to help us keep the Ten Commandments: the Father gives us all creation, Christ all his works, the Holy Spirit all his gifts.[5]

The Creed is doxological; it praises the Father who gives us knowledge of His grace and mercy in His Son, which the Holy Spirit delivers to us in the word of the faith-creating Gospel.

4   Albrecht Peters, *Creed*, trans. Thomas H. Trapp, *Commentary on Luther's Catechisms* 2 (St. Louis: Concordia, 2011), 7.

5   LC II 67–69; K-W 440. Albrecht Peters captures Luther's intention: "One needs to maintain that the center of the catechism is the interpretation of the Creed as it moves from creation to redemption all the way to sanctification. Justification's 'by grace alone' is hinted at already in the First Article: the heavenly Father gives to the confessor His blessing as Creator 'out of fatherly, divine goodness and mercy without any merit or worthiness in me.' This 'by grace alone' is anchored in the 'Jesus Christ alone' of the Second Article: 'Jesus Christ [is] my Lord who has redeemed me, a lost and condemned creature.' Both reach their completion in the 'by faith alone' of the Third Article: I cannot, 'by my own reason or strength,' believe in Jesus Christ as my Lord and Redeemer. This takes place only by virtue of the office and work of the Holy Spirit" (*Ten Commandments*, 46).

THE FIRST ARTICLE

Creation
I believe in God, the Father Almighty,
Maker of heaven and earth.

What does this mean?
I believe that God has made me and all creatures; that He has
given me my body and soul, eyes, ears, and all my members,
my reason and all my senses, and still takes care of them.

He also gives me clothing and shoes, food and drink,
house and home, wife and children, land, animals,
and all I have. He richly and daily provides me with
all that I need to support this body and life.

He defends me against all danger and guards
and protects me from all evil.

All this He does only out of fatherly, divine goodness and
mercy, without any merit or worthiness in me. For all this
it is my duty to thank and praise, serve and obey Him.

This is most certainly true.

   Almighty Maker of heaven and earth: We give You thanks for the gift of
our creation in body and soul. You are the giver of eyes, ears, and all our members. You have endowed us with our reason and senses, and in Your mercy You
take care of us. For what we need to support this body and life—food and
drink, house and home, wife and children, land and animals, and all that we
have—You richly and daily provide. In Your kind care You defend us against all
danger and guard and protect us from all evil. All this You do out of fatherly,
divine goodness and mercy, without any merit or worthiness in us. So we implore You, gracious God, to give us faith to acknowledge Your benefits, tongues
to thank and praise Your holy name, and lives joyfully given to serve and obey

You; through Jesus Christ, Your Son, who lives and reigns with You and the Holy Spirit, one God forever. Amen.

—◦◦◦—

Luther's basic structural design of his explanation of the First Article might be expressed in this way according to Oswald Bayer:[6]

> **Faith:** "I believe. . . .
>
> **Giver:** "God, the Father Almighty, Maker of heaven and earth."
>
> **Gift:** "God has made me and all creatures . . . He has given me . . . and still takes care of them. . . . He also gives me clothing and shoes, food and drink . . . all that I need to support this body and life. . . . He defends . . . guards and protects . . . ."
>
> **Giver:** "All this He does only out of fatherly, divine goodness and mercy, without any merit or worthiness in me."
>
> **Response:** "For all this it is my duty to thank and praise, serve and obey Him."
>
> **Faith:** "This is most certainly true."

The explanation begins and ends with faith as both Giver and gift are confessed, and the response of the creature in lip and life is anticipated. Embraced within this confession of faith is the confidence that God has created me along with all creatures. Luther personalizes this confession; it is not merely that God is a distant architect of the universe or a primal cause and source of all things, but He is *my Father* and He has made *me* along with all creatures. Through these creatures He has created and continues to sustain my life. Oswald Bayer puts it like this: "Since God has called me and all creatures into existence, he does not leave me alone; he makes sure that I am together with the other creatures. . . . [I]n fact I come *through* them—most especially: through my parents. The fellow creatures are the medium, God works through them; they are 'the means, through

---

6   See Oswald Bayer, *Martin Luther's Theology: A Contemporary Interpretation*, trans. Thomas H. Trapp (Grand Rapids: Eerdmans, 2008), 163.

which God gives everything.' "[7] Praying the Creed does not allow us to forget that "creatures are the gloves on God's hands."[8]

Luther's explanation captures the inclusiveness of bodily gifts ("He has given me my body . . . and all my senses) as coming from the Father and being preserved by Him, as well as the distribution of creaturely gifts of daily bread ("clothing and shoes . . . and all I have"). Human beings are the recipients of God's fatherly defense, guardianship, and protection from all evil.

God does everything out of "fatherly, divine goodness and mercy, without any merit or worthiness in me." Here it is instructive to note the observation of Oswald Bayer that the phrase "without any merit or worthiness in me" expresses the doctrine of justification in the First Article.[9]

Luther comments in a house postil for Pentecost Monday 1534:

> Giving when it proceeds from true love, makes the gift all the greater and more precious; as we are wont to say, it makes me happy, for it is a gift of love, if I know that the heart is in it. On the other hand, if we doubt the existence of heartfelt love, we do not think very highly of the gift. If, therefore, God had given us only one eye, one foot, or one hand, and we were convinced that he had done this out of divine, fatherly love, then such eye, foot, or hand would be dearer to us than if there had been a thousand eyes, feet, or hands.[10]

The First Article focuses our attention not simply on the creaturely gifts but on the Creator whose fatherly goodness stands behind these gifts. Seeing the gifts in light of the Father who gives them without any merit or worthiness on the part of the recipient magnifies their value. They are acknowledged as benefactions from the bounty of a gracious God and so are received with thanksgiving.

---

7   Bayer, *Luther's Theology*, 167.

8   Arand, Kolb, and Nestingen, *The Lutheran Confessions: History and Theology*, 54.

9   Bayer: "Luther's Small Catechism does not begin to use the explicit terminology of justification only when it arrives at the explanation of the second or the third article of the Apostles' Creed, which is what one would expect to be the case; it surprisingly appears already in the explanation to the first article, the article that deals with creation" (*Luther's Theology*, 95). Also see Robert Kolb: "Not only as a sinner but as a creature human beings bring nothing to God. They receive their identity, their continued existence, their righteousness from him, Almighty, Father, Creator" (*Martin Luther: Confessor of the Faith* [Oxford: Oxford University Press, 2009], 105).

10   *Sermons of Martin Luther: The House Postils*, trans. Eugene Klug (Grand Rapids: Baker, 1996), 2:196–97.

Albrecht Peters writes of Luther's explanation of the First Article of the Apostles' Creed in the Small Catechism:

> The scope of the article is framed with a view toward God: The Christian person, who is called into existence under the First Commandment, gives an account of his faith and confesses: "My God and father, the creator of the heavens and the earth, has made me."[11]

The God confessed in the First Article of the Christian Creed is no nameless deity; He is the God and Father of our Lord Jesus Christ. No abstract force, this God who is at once both Father and Almighty. It is only in and through the Son that we know God to be our Father.[12]

In its entirety, Luther's confession of the First Article is grounded in the truth that God is the Father Almighty who has created everything that exists. This confession embraces the personal ("has made me"), the cosmic/universal ("and all creatures"), the communal ("He also gives me . . . house and home, wife and children, land, animals, and all I have"), the providential ("He defends me against all danger and guards and protects me from all evil"), and the doxological ("For all this it is my duty to thank and praise, serve and obey Him"). All this is so because God is the Father Almighty who has created all things and continues to uphold His creation.

It is only in and through the Son that we know God to be our Father.

The First Article presupposes the Second Article. The fatherhood of God is not a metaphorical description of God's kindness. Rather, it expresses the fact that this God is the Father of Jesus and the source of all things. God can be called "Father" only by those who are in the Son. "For in Christ Jesus you are all sons of God, though faith" (Galatians 3:26), and so are enlivened to call God Father. "For you did not receive the spirit of slavery to fall back into fear, but you have received the Spirit of adoption as sons, by whom we cry, 'Abba! Father!' " (Romans 8:15).

The God who is our Father is almighty. His omnipotence is not an abstraction. "Back of what God does as Father is his omnipotence. Omnipotence means above

11   Peters, *Creed*, 62.

12   Here see Luther's comments in his *Confession Concerning Christ's Supper*, written a year prior to the catechism, in 1528: "These are the three persons and one God, who has given himself to us all wholly and completely, with all that he is and has. The Father gives himself to us, with heaven and earth and all the creatures, in order that they may serve us and benefit us. But this gift has become obscured and useless through Adam's fall. Therefore the Son himself subsequently gave himself and bestowed all his works, sufferings, wisdom, and righteousness, and reconciled us to the Father, in order that restored to life and righteousness, we might also know and have the Father and his gifts" (AE 37:366).

all that God is the lord of life and death, of my life and my death."[13] The Father is almighty. That is to say, He alone is Lord over all that He has made. "When omnipotence is denied, God himself gets denied."[14] He is not simply one power among many. He is Lord, as described by Isaiah: "I am the LORD, and there is no other, besides Me there is no God; I equip you, though you do not know Me, that people may know, from the rising of the sun and from the west, that there is none besides Me; I am the LORD, and there is no other. I form light and create darkness, I make well-being and create calamity, I am the LORD, who does all these things" (Isaiah 45:5–7). The heavenly liturgy echoes the ceaseless Sanctus: "Holy, holy, holy, is the Lord God Almighty, who was and is and is to come!" (Revelation 4:8). Past and future are under His lordship. There is nothing here of a Deity whose power is evolving only to come to culmination in some future aeon. He is the Lord who works all things by necessity, to paraphrase Luther.[15]

Herbert Girgensohn notes that the confession of God as almighty "is directed against two basic sins, *superbia* and *diffidentia,* pride and despair."[16] That is to say, this confession at once humbles us and consoles us.

The confession of God's omnipotence is devastating to the pride that would act as if God did not exist or that we are autonomous beings, living independent of our Creator. To say that God is almighty is, in fact, to recognize that He is Lord and not we. By His Word, He brought us into existence, creating us body and soul. By His Word, He will return us to dust, as Psalm 90 attests: "You return man to dust and say, 'Return, O children of man!' " (Psalm 90:3). The God to whom we pray is the Lord over life and death; nothing is removed from His dominion.

But to those sunk in despair because of their failure to fear, love, and trust in God above all things, the confession that the Father is almighty is pure consolation. Here is a God who has the power to save, and He is my Father for the sake of His Son. This power to save is frequently referenced in the Holy Scriptures, particularly in the Psalms. As Oswald Bayer puts it: "The certainty of the love of God is the certainty of this love's omnipotence, which is able to overcome all powers that would stand against it."[17] That which God promises, He can do. The

---

13 Herbert Girgensohn, *Teaching Luther's Catechism*, 1:133.

14 Oswald Bayer, "God's Omnipotence," *Lutheran Quarterly* 23, no. 1 (Spring 2009): 87.

15 See Luther's *Bondage of the Will* (1525), AE 33:43, where Luther writes against Erasmus, whose assertions of human freedom would undermine God's omnipotence and thus rob Christians of the certainty of God's promise in Romans 8:28 to work *all* things for the good of those who have been called according to His purpose.

16 Girgensohn, *Teaching Luther's Catechism*, 1:134.

17 Bayer, "God's Omnipotence," 86.

God who calls into existence things that are not is the Lord whose almightiness is steadfast and trustworthy. The apostle Paul references this in Romans in his discourse on Abraham's faith. He says that God "gives life to the dead and calls into existence the things that do not exist" (Romans 4:17). Thus Bayer observes that "Luther clings to God's fatherly goodness, to his omnipotence and simultaneously to his oneness, and this he does for the sake of the certainty of salvation."[18] It is only through the message of Jesus' death and resurrection that we know God's omnipotence as good news for sinners.

The First Article anticipates the explanation to the Fourth Petition of the Lord's Prayer, "Give us this day our daily bread." It also anticipates especially the Daily Prayers and Table of Duties appended by Luther to the Six Chief Parts of Christian Doctrine. The first stanza of the reformer's creedal hymn summarizes the teaching of the catechism, teaching us to acknowledge the Father as the Creator and look to Him for every good:

> We all believe in one true God,
>> Who created earth and heaven,
> The Father, who to us in love
>> Has the right of children given.
> He in soul and body feeds us;
>> All we need His hand provides us;
> Through all snares and perils leads us,
>> Watching that no harm betide us.
> He cares for us by day and night;
> All things are governed by His might. (*LSB* 954:1)

THE SECOND ARTICLE

Redemption
And in Jesus Christ, His only Son, our Lord, who was
conceived by the Holy Spirit, born of the Virgin Mary,
suffered under Pontius Pilate, was crucified, died and was buried.
He descended into hell. The third day He rose again from

---

18   Bayer, "God's Omnipotence," 99.

the dead. He ascended into heaven and sits at the
right hand of God, the Father Almighty. From thence
He will come to judge the living and the dead.

What does this mean?

I believe that Jesus Christ, true God, begotten of the Father from
eternity, and also true man, born of the Virgin Mary, is my Lord,

who has redeemed me, a lost and condemned person,
purchased and won me from all sins, from death, and from the
power of the devil; not with gold or silver, but with His holy,
precious blood and with His innocent suffering and death,

that I may be His own and live under Him
in His kingdom and serve Him in everlasting
righteousness, innocence, and blessedness,

just as He is risen from the dead, lives and reigns to all eternity.

This is most certainly true.

Lord Jesus Christ, true God, begotten of the Father from all eternity, and true man, born of the Virgin Mary, You have redeemed us lost and condemned persons. For purchasing and winning us from all sin, from death, and from the power of the devil, not with gold or silver but with Your holy, precious blood and with Your innocent suffering and death, we give You thanks. We praise You that You have made us Your own so that we may live under You in Your kingdom and serve You in everlasting righteousness, innocence, and blessedness, just as You are risen from the dead and live and reign to all eternity with Your Father and the Holy Spirit, one God, now and forever. Amen.

The structure of the Second Article parallels that of the First Article:

Faith: "I believe . . ."

Giver: "Jesus Christ, true God . . ."

Gift: "who has redeemed me . . ."

Response: "so that I may . . . live under Him in His kingdom and serve Him"

Faith: "This is most certainly true."[19]

The Second Article of the Creed is an expansion of the foundational New Testament confession "Jesus is Lord" (cf. John 20:28; 1 Corinthians 12:3; Philippians 2:11; etc.). Luther identifies this confession as the heart of the Second Article:

> Here we get to know the second person of the Godhead, and we see what we have from God over and above the temporal goods mentioned above, namely, how he has given himself completely to us, withholding nothing. This article is very rich and far-reaching, but in order to treat it briefly for children, we shall take up one phrase and in it grasp the substance of the article so that everyone may learn from it, as we have said, how we are redeemed. We shall concentrate on these words, "in Jesus Christ, our Lord."[20]

For Luther, the entirety of Christ's person and work are encapsulated in the title "Lord," as he points out in the Large Catechism: "Let this be the summary of this article, that the little word 'Lord' simply means the same as Redeemer, that is, he who has brought us back from the devil to God, from death to life, from sin to righteousness, and keeps us there."[21] The second stanza of the hymn summarizes the person and work of our Lord Jesus Christ who took on flesh to be our Redeemer:

> **We all believe in Jesus Christ,**
> **His own Son, our Lord, possessing**
> **An equal Godhead, throne, and might,**
> **Source of ev'ry grace and blessing;**
> **Born of Mary, virgin mother,**
> **By the power of the Spirit,**
> **Word made flesh, our elder brother;**
> **That the lost might life inherit,**

---

19   See Bayer, *Luther's Theology*, 230–31.

20   LC II 26; K-W 434.

21   LC II 31; K-W 434.

Was crucified for all our sin
And raised by God to life again. (*LSB* 954:2)

Jesus is confessed as Lord. As we have seen from Luther's treatment of the First Commandment, no human being is without a lord of one kind or another. If you are not under the lordship of Jesus Christ, you will be under the lordship of sin, death, and the devil. To say "Jesus is my Lord" does not mean that we make Him the Lord of our lives. As Mark Seifrid helpfully puts it: "It is not in our power to choose that lord. We do not *make* Christ our Lord. Rather, God in grace has *given* us Christ as our *saving* Lord: we have been liberated from sin and enslaved to righteousness."[22] To have Christ as Lord is to have a God who saves from every other lord who would enslave and bring death.

> *If you are not under the lordship of Jesus Christ, you will be under the lordship of sin, death, and the devil.*

The Creed does not hold up Christ as a model to be emulated or as a teacher whose instruction will enable human beings to develop their full moral or religious capacities. As Klaus Schwarzwäller wisely puts it: "Whoever knows the Old Testament or anything about ancient Judaism knows that we did not need another model in Jesus: there were already examples enough."[23] Jesus is unique. To confess His lordship is to assert that this man is the God who saves us.

It is from the central confession of the lordship of Jesus Christ that Luther unfolds the totality of the Second Article. Jesus is "true God, begotten of the Father from eternity" and at the same time "true man, born of the Virgin Mary." With concise simplicity these words summarize the Christology of the two natures in Christ. The one who is both true God and true man is "my Lord." Once again, we see how Luther personalizes the dogmatic truth of Jesus' humanity and deity. "God has *really entered* humanity and the infinite has actually *come down into* the finite."[24] And He has done it for me!

In other words, this confession of the divine and human natures in the one person of Jesus Christ is driven by soteriology, that is, by the saving work of Christ, "who has redeemed me, a lost and condemned person." Luther uses two

---

22   Mark Seifrid, "Romans 7: The Voice of the Law, the Cry of Lament, and the Shout of Thanksgiving," in *Perspectives on Our Struggle with Sin: 3 Views of Romans 7,* ed. Terry L. Wilder (Nashville: B&H Academic, 2011), 130.

23   Klaus Schwarzwäller, *Cross and Resurrection: God's Wonder and Mystery,* trans. Mark Mattes and Ken Sundet Jones (Minneapolis: Fortress, 2012), 86.

24   Hermann Sasse, *Here We Stand,* trans. Theodore G. Tappert (Adelaide, Australia: Lutheran Publishing House, 1979), 153.

descriptive words to denote our status apart from Christ Jesus: "lost and condemned." In this way he vividly paints the condition of alienation from the Creator ("lost") and life as one who is guilty, that is, who is facing a death sentence. Jesus' work of redemption is not enacted in an economic transaction of gold or silver (see 1 Peter 1:18) but through His "holy, precious blood and with His innocent suffering and death." Luther describes this work of redemption using both the language of vicarious atonement ("purchased") and that of Jesus' victory over the powers that condemn and hold captive ("won"). This is given further explication in the Large Catechism:

> There was no counsel, no help, no comfort for us until this only and eternal Son of God, in his unfathomable goodness, had mercy on us because of our misery and distress and came from heaven to help us. Those tyrants and jailers have now been routed, and their place has been taken by Jesus Christ, the Lord of life, righteousness, and every good and blessing. He has snatched us, poor lost creatures, from the jaws of hell, won us, made us free, and restored us to the Father's favor and grace. As his own possession he has taken us under his protection and shelter, in order that he may rule us by his righteousness, wisdom, power, life, and blessedness.[25]

In Jesus' sacrificial death, He has defeated the enemies that would destroy us—sin, death, and the devil. In their place He provides us with forgiveness of sin, life, and salvation.

The outcome of this redeeming work is seen in Luther's assertion that Christ possesses the believer: "that I may be His own and live under Him in His kingdom and serve Him in everlasting righteousness, innocence, and blessedness." Under the ownership of the Lord Christ, the believer is covered by His righteousness, is innocent through the imputation of this righteousness, and thus is blessed to have life in communion with God and to serve Him not as a slave but as a child.

> Christ's lordship encompasses my existence in the here and now, not only from the then and there of the offering upon Golgotha, but simultaneously from the here and now of His on-going lordship, and it opens to me the future of a life in God that overcomes death. The here and now of my existence, which is confined to the earth, has all the strictures of such an existence removed eschatologically in

---

25   LC II 29–30; K-W 434.

this way; already now, in Him, even though still hidden under the cross of Jesus and open only to the eyes of faith, the final lordship that Christ is to exercise in the Kingdom of God begins to dawn.[26]

In Christ, we now live by faith even as we wait in hope for that day when faith will give way to sight and we will see Him as He is. In the meantime, the Second Article tutors us to pray the final prayer recorded in the Book of Revelation: "Amen. Come, Lord Jesus!" (Revelation 22:20).

THE THIRD ARTICLE

Sanctification
I believe in the Holy Spirit, the holy Christian church,
the communion of saints, the forgiveness of sins, the
resurrection of the body, and the life everlasting. Amen.

What does this mean?
I believe that I cannot by my own reason or strength
believe in Jesus Christ, my Lord, or come to Him; but the
Holy Spirit has called me by the Gospel, enlightened me
with His gifts, sanctified and kept me in the true faith.

In the same way He calls, gathers, enlightens, and
sanctifies the whole Christian church on earth, and
keeps it with Jesus Christ in the one true faith.

In this Christian church He daily and richly forgives
all my sins and the sins of all believers.

On the Last Day He will raise me and all the dead, and
give eternal life to me and all believers in Christ.

This is most certainly true.

---

26   Peters, *Creed*, 144. See also Sasse: "Only on the basis of the resurrection message can the confession by understood that Jesus Christ is Lord" ("Jesus Christ Is Lord," 21).

Lord Jesus, we cannot believe in You by our own reason or strength or come to You, but Your Holy Spirit has called us by the Gospel, enlightened us with His gifts, sanctified and kept us in the true faith. In the same way He calls, gathers, enlightens, and sanctifies the whole Christian Church on earth and keeps it with You in the one true faith. In this Christian Church, the Holy Spirit daily and richly forgives us all our sins. On the Last Day, He will raise all the dead and give all of us who believe in You eternal life. For this we praise You and implore You according to Your promise to send us the Comforter that we might continue firm in this confession. For You live and reign with Him and the Father, one God, now and forever. Amen.

———————— ⟶∘⟨⟩∘⟵ ————————

With Luther's explanation of the Third Article, the structure is modified. Here Luther does not begin with faith but with the inability to believe, and in place of a "response" there is the "outcome" of the Spirit's work:

Confession of inability: "I believe that I cannot . . ."

Giver: "but the Holy Spirit has called me . . ."

Gift: ". . . enlightened me with His gifts, sanctified and kept me in the true faith . . ."

Outcome: "On the Last Day . . ."

Faith: "This is most certainly true."[27]

The flow of the Third Article is from the Holy Spirit through the Son and to the Father. It is the Holy Spirit who calls us through the Gospel to faith in the Son so we might have forgiveness of sins, resurrection of the body, and life everlasting with the Father. "Luther summarizes the external activity of the Spirit by using one key word: Gospel."[28] It is only through this Gospel, the Good News of the forgiveness of sins for the sake of Christ, that the Spirit works to bring sinners to God and to give them the confidence to call God "Father." The Third Article guards prayer against what Luther called "enthusiasm" or the search for a God within. As

> The Third Article guards prayer against what Luther called "enthusiasm" or the search for a God within.

---

27   See Bayer, *Luther's Theology*, 240ff.

28   Peters, *Creed*, 241.

Oswald Bayer warns: "Those who want to search for the Holy Spirit deep inside themselves, in a realm too deep for words to express, will find ghosts, not God."[29]

The Third Article of the Creed is understood in relationship to the Second Article.

> The question the second article left unanswered was: How is it possible to gain access to the reality described in this article? . . . The third article answers the question left unanswered in the second article: We gain access to Jesus Christ and his world through the Holy Spirit.[30]

In the words of the apostle Paul, "no one can say 'Jesus is Lord' except in the Holy Spirit" (1 Corinthians 12:3). In the Large Catechism, Luther echoes Paul:

> Neither you nor I could ever know anything about Christ, or believe in him and receive him as Lord, unless these were offered to us and bestowed on our hearts through the preaching of the gospel by the Holy Spirit. The work is finished and completed; Christ has acquired and won the treasure for us by his sufferings, death, and resurrection, etc. But if the work remained hidden so that no one knew of it, it would have been all in vain, all lost. In order that this treasure might not remain buried but be put to use and enjoyed, God has caused the Word to be published and proclaimed, in which he has given the Holy Spirit to offer and apply to us this treasure, this redemption. Therefore being made holy is nothing else than bringing us to the Lord Christ to receive this blessing, to which we could not have come by ourselves.[31]

---

29   Bayer, *Theology the Lutheran Way*, 55.

30   Girgensohn, *Teaching Luther's Catechism*, 1:177. Also note Sasse: "The New Testament's view of the Holy Spirit can be stated in one sentence: Where Christ is, there is the Holy Spirit; where the Holy Spirit is, there is Christ. Christ and the Holy Spirit belong together. Faith can have no experience of the reality of the Holy Spirit unless it is somehow also an experience of the true and living presence of Christ. There can be no faith in the present Christ, no confession that Jesus is Lord, unless it is mediated through the Holy Spirit" ("Jesus Christ Is Lord," 31).

31   LC II 38–39; K-W 436. Also note: "We are not our own creator and preserver, lord and redeemer, cannot justify, sanctify, or awaken ourselves from the dead. The turn of phrase from the First Article 'all without my merits and worthiness' is taken up in the Third Article with the words 'not by my own reason or strength'; both phrases serve as a bridge and are held together by the broad arch that stretches from the creation to the new creation" (Peters, *Creed*, 235).

We can only call on the name of the Lord in prayer because the Spirit has first called us by the Gospel to faith in Christ Jesus.

Without the Spirit's work in the Gospel, we cannot by our own reason or strength come to Christ. Here, because he sets the phrase in the present tense, Luther is not limiting the Spirit's work to conversion or to the initial coming to faith. I could not believe much less pray for even a moment were it not for the Holy Spirit who continues to work faith and preserve me in this faith through the word of the cross.

The Third Article comforts Christians who struggle to pray as it reminds us that faith is not grounded in the self but in the sure and certain work of the Holy Spirit, who brings us to confess Christ by the potency of the Gospel. As Jeffrey Silcock puts it: "Strictly speaking, Christians do not 'possess' the Spirit, but the Spirit 'possesses' them." [32] This is the comfort beyond all telling of which Luther has us sing:

> We all confess the Holy Ghost,
>> Who, in highest heaven dwelling
> With God the Father and the Son,
>> Comforts us beyond all telling;
> Who the Church, His own creation,
>> Keeps in unity of spirit.
> Here forgiveness and salvation
>> Daily come through Jesus' merit.
> All flesh shall rise, and we shall be
> In bliss with God eternally. (*LSB* 954:3)

"Luther's whole exposition of the Creed proceeds in terms of divine giving."[33] The Spirit enlightens us with His gifts so that we confess the treasures of redemption procured by the Son and in Him rejoice in the riches of the Father's favor expressed in all of His provisions for body and soul. In this way Luther teaches us to pray each article of the Creed in praise and thanksgiving to the triune God.

---

32   Jeffrey Silcock, "Luther on the Holy Spirit and His Use of God's Word," in *The Oxford Handbook of Martin Luther's Theology*, ed. Robert Kolb, Irene Dingel, L'ubomír Batka (Oxford: Oxford University Press, 2014), 305.

33   Risto Saainen, "Luther and *Beneficia*," in *The Reformation as Christianization: Essays on Scott Hendrix's Christianization Thesis*, ed. Anna Marie Johnson and John A. Maxfield (Tübingen: Mohr Siebeck, 2012), 180.

CHAPTER 4

The Lord's Prayer

Prayer Under the Pressure of the Cross

Nowhere is it more evident that the catechism can be prayed than in Luther's exposition of the Lord's Prayer. "All true prayer finds the seed around which it can crystalize in the Lord's Prayer."[1] The Lord's Prayer is both the source and norm of all Christian praying.[2] From the Lord's Prayer all other petitions, intercessions, supplications, and thanksgivings are derived. At the same time, the Lord's Prayer serves to govern all for which the Christian prays, distinguishing true prayers based on the Lord's commands and promises from false prayers grounded in sinful desire and arising in contradiction to the Word of God. Such prayer is prompted by the Holy Spirit: "Wherever there is a Christian, there is none other than the Holy Spirit, who does nothing but pray without ceasing. . . . A Christian without prayer is just as impossible as a living person without a pulse."[3]

The Lord's Prayer is God's Word to us, and as this word is received by faith it becomes our words to God. As Helmut Thielicke points out: "Prayer is not our action but our reaction. It bases itself on the preceding Word of God which makes it

---

1   Albrecht Peters, *Lord's Prayer*, 4.

2   Here see Peters: "The Lord's Prayer for [Luther] serves as norm, which wishes to control the material content of our prayers" (*Lord's Prayer*, 29). Also see Bruce G. McNair: "For Luther, the Lord's Prayer was the most important prayer a believer could pray, and he considered this prayer so important that he thought every other prayer should express the content and meaning of the Lord's Prayer" ("Luther and the Pastoral Theology of the Lord's Prayer," *Logia* 14, no. 4 [Reformation 2005]: 41). For a helpful overview of Luther's theology and practice of prayer as it is centered in the Lord's Prayer, see Martin E. Lehmann, *Luther and Prayer* (Milwaukee: Northwestern, 1985).

3   *Sermons on John 14–16* (1533–34/1538–39), AE 24:89.

possible."[4] This is why Luther puts so much stock in the Lord's Prayer. Because this prayer is given to us by Christ, when we utter its petitions we may be certain that God is pleased with what we ask for because He has taught us to pray in this way.

In a sermon on the Gospel of John, Luther summarized the structure and content of the Lord's Prayer:

> God Himself has established the order in the Lord's Prayer and has specified three goals which must always have precedence: that His name be hallowed, His kingdom, and His will. . . . Preference must be given to God's name and to His kingdom; if this is done, then our interests will surely follow. . . . These last four parts of the Lord's Prayer, which pertain to the temporal needs of our life, are surely also included in His will. But the three items that are specifically His own have priority. . . . And if you pray in this way, asking His will be done, your prayer is certainly heard. But your prayer must be offered so as not to violate or reverse God's order or ignore the most important matters.[5]

The catechism's explanation of the Lord's Prayer begins with the Father's tender invitation to pray and ends with the command and promise of God. As it is diagrammed below, the "command and promise" parallel the Decalogue and the Creed, thus drawing the first three parts of the catechism together:

LORD'S PRAYER	DECALOGUE/CREED
Introduction	First Commandment/First Article
First Petition	Second Commandment
Second Petition	Second & Third Articles
Third Petition	Third Article
Fourth Petition	Ninth & Tenth Commandments/First Article
Fifth Petition	Third Article
Sixth Petition	Second Article
Seventh Petition	First, Second, Third Articles
Conclusion	"This is most certainly true."

---

4   Helmut Thielicke, *The Evangelical Faith*, trans. Geoffrey W. Bromiley (Grand Rapids: Eerdmans, 1982), 3:84.

5   *Sermons on John 14–16* (1533–34/1538–39), AE 24:321.

Luther's theology of prayer is a reflection of the theology of the cross.

The Ten Commandments set out the requirements of creaturely life, incumbent by creation; the Creed declares the gifts of the Triune God; the Lord's Prayer gives voice to the circumstances of the believer living in the world of the *nomos* (law) in the hope of the gospel. . . . Luther's explanations of the Lord's Prayer arise from such an analysis of the situation of faith. Barraged by the relentless demands of the law, under assault by the powers of this age yet gripped in the hope of the gospel, the believer learns "where to seek and obtain that aid." So, while exposing the Lord's Prayer at its first level, as instruction in how to pray, Luther is at the same time describing the contention in which faith lives, giving language for the rhythm of death and resurrection that is the hallmark of life in Christ. At this level, the Lord's Prayer is a cry wrung from the crucible, an exposition of the shape of life lived under the sign of the cross in the hope of the resurrection.[6]

Each petition of the Lord's Prayer is a diagnosis of our neediness and a promise of God's mercy.[7]

The Introduction
Our Father who art in heaven.

Our Father in heaven.

What does this mean?
With these words God tenderly invites us to believe
that He is our true Father and that we are His true
children, so that with all boldness and confidence we
may ask Him as dear children ask their dear father.

---

6   James A. Nestingen, "The Lord's Prayer in Luther's Catechism," *Word & World* 22, no. 1 (Winter 2002): 38, 40. Used with permission. All rights reserved.

7   In his *Exposition of the Lord's Prayer* (1519), Luther described the Lord's Prayer as "seven reminders of our wretchedness and poverty by means of which man, led to a knowledge of self, can see what a miserable and perilous life he leads here on earth" (AE 42:27).

Holy Father, with Your words You tenderly invite us to believe that You are our true Father and we are Your true children. Give us boldness and confidence to trust Your promises and so petition You as dear children addressing their dear father; through Jesus Christ, our Lord. Amen.

The antiphonal-like conclusion at the end of each of Luther's explanations of the three articles of the Creed—"This is most certainly true"—constitutes the platform upon which prayer stands. God can be addressed as Father with "boldness and confidence" exclusively because of the redeeming work of the Son and only through the work of the Holy Spirit who calls to faith by the Gospel. "Only that prayer which places itself deep within God's command and promise is welcome in the presence of the holy majesty and is heard."[8] Christian prayer is based on the reality that God is our Father. This gives us boldness and confidence in our praying. God's promise (*promissio Dei*) is foundational and primary for prayer.[9] Our desperate neediness drives us to prayer, but it is God's command and promise which are the basis for our praying. Without them, our prayer would be a futile exercise. Likewise, faith does not constitute prayer, but without trust in God's promise, true prayer is impossible. In the imperiled existence that is our lot in this fallen world, where the gravitational pull of our flesh is constantly separating us from God's command and promise, and where the devil is ever on the attack, faith, Oswald Bayer writes, "is rather the courage to endure the old world and call upon

Our desperate neediness drives us to prayer, but it is God's command and promise which are the basis for our praying.

8   Peters, *Lord's Prayer*, 15.

9   Oswald Bayer writes: "The promise of God [*promissio Dei*], which is the foundation on which the entire prayer relies: if there were no promise, our prayer would be worthless; it would be unworthy of a favorable hearing, since it would rely on its own merit" (*Luther's Theology*, 347). Also see M. Haemig: "He [Luther] asserted that Christians pray because God has commanded them to pray and has promised to hear them. For this reason, Christians pray to God, not Mary or the saints. Prayer was the proper response to God; it never originated the relationship with God. Luther rejected the idea that prayer was a good work and rejected practices—such as repetition of prayers and the use of prayers for works of satisfaction—that might lead to the idea that prayer was a good work. Prayer was not based on the Christian's worthiness to pray. Need drives her to prayer, and she brings all her needs to God, trusting God's promise to hear her" (cited by Carter Lindberg in "Piety, Prayer, and Worship in Luther's View of Daily Life," in *The Oxford Handbook of Martin Luther's Theology*, ed. Robert Kolb, Irene Dingel, L'ubomír Batka [Oxford: Oxford University Press, 2014], 418).

God, certain that God will hear and answer even though he may at times seem not to do so."[10]

Just as the First Commandment and the First Article of the Creed interlock, so both are brought to focus in the catechism's Introduction to the Lord's Prayer. The God who is to be feared, loved, and trusted above all things is none other than God, the Father Almighty, Maker of heaven and earth. It is this God—the Father of our Lord Jesus Christ—who is addressed in prayer. Prayer is an entitlement given to children of God. In Jesus Christ, the fatherly heart of God is laid bare. Apart from the revelation of His divine mercy and compassion, His steadfast love and grace in Christ Jesus, we would be left in uncertainty when it comes to God's attitude toward us. In Christ we know that God is our true Father and we are His true children, thus we can "call Him Father with delight," to use the language of the Pentecost hymn.[11] We are His dear children, and He is a dear Father.

The Lord's Prayer is prayed with boldness and confidence, for it is uttered in the knowledge that God is our true God and we are His true children.[12] Positively, it is the supplication that dear children make of a dear father. Negatively, it is prayed against Satan, the old evil foe who would like nothing better than to deprive us of our status as sons of God and capture us to perish as his children. Thus Albrecht Peters notes: "The reformer never backs down from this thesis that God through the Lord's Prayer desires to open our eyes to the abyss in which normally we carelessly and foolishly live from day to day."[13] The Lord's Prayer is in the hearts and on the tongues of Christians who are under attack, constantly bombarded by attacks of the evil one, drawn by the irresistible desires of the flesh, and stumbling amid the hazards of life in this fallen world. It is a prayer prayed by those who are weak and defenseless against enemies who are far too crafty and more potent than flesh and blood.[14] But it is addressed to the God who is truth, who is not only our almighty Creator but also our Father. Little wonder that the great German-American catechist J. Michel Reu called Luther's Introduction to

---

10   Oswald Bayer, *Living by Faith,* trans. Geoffrey W. Bromiley (Grand Rapids: Eerdmans, 2003), 77.

11   "Come, Holy Ghost, God and Lord," *LSB* 497:2.

12   This theme is present in two of Luther's writings from 1519: *Exposition of the Lord's Prayer* (AE 42:15–81) and *On Rogationtide Prayer and Procession* (AE 42:83–93). In this latter essay, Luther references Matthew 21:22; Mark 11:24; and Luke 11:9–13 to conclude that "we should cheerfully rely on these and similar promises and commands and pray with true confidence" (AE 42:88).

13   Peters, *Lord's Prayer,* 9.

14   Note Luther in the Large Catechism: "This we must know, that all our safety and protection consists in prayer alone. For we are far too weak against the devil and all his might and forces arrayed against us, trying to trample us underfoot" (LC III 30; K-W 444).

the Lord's Prayer "the most beautiful part of his exposition of the Lord's Prayer—in the sunburst of the catechism one of the most resplendent gems."[15] Luther's words, tender with intimacy, draw the believer to speak with the Father in confident faith even in the presence of enemies within and without.

To pray "*our* Father" is to be drawn out of one's self-enclosed life, a "me and God" existence, to make intercession for the household of the Father and extending outward to include the whole world. "Think," says Luther, "that the whole of Christendom, all devout Christians, are standing there beside you and you are standing among them in a common, united petition which God cannot disdain."[16] The Lord's Prayer is an expansive prayer as it encompasses supplication for all people. Indeed, as Georg Vicedom says, "He who prays the Our Father should always have the world map before his eyes!"[17]

The First Petition
Hallowed be Thy name.

Hallowed be Your name.

What does this mean?
God's name is certainly holy in itself, but we pray in this
petition that it may be kept holy among us also.

How is God's name kept holy?
God's name is kept holy when the Word of God is taught in its
truth and purity, and we, as the children of God, also lead holy
lives according to it. Help us to do this, dear Father in heaven!
But anyone who teaches or lives contrary to God's Word profanes
the name of God among us. Protect us from this, heavenly Father!

Heavenly Father, whose name alone is holy in itself, by Your grace grant
that it may be kept holy among us also. Cause Your Word to be taught in truth

---

15   J. Michel Reu, *Catechetics* (Chicago: Wartburg Press, 1927), 106.

16   *Simple Way to Pray* (1535), AE 43:198.

17   Georg Vicedom, *A Prayer for the World*, trans. Edward and Marie Schroeder (St. Louis: Concordia, 1967), 81.

and purity in our midst, and sanctify us by Your truth to live holy lives according to it. Protect us from false teaching and unholy living that would profane Your name among us; through Jesus Christ, Your Son, who lives and reigns with You and the Holy Spirit, ever one God. Amen.

In *Exposition of the Lord's Prayer*, the reformer presents this petition as the key to praying the Lord's Prayer: "That is why I just called this first petition an unlimited one, the foremost one, encompassing all the others. If anyone were able to hallow God's name perfectly, he would no longer need to pray the Lord's Prayer."[18]

Luther's exposition of the First Petition hearkens back to the Second Commandment. The opposite of the misuse of God's name is the hallowing of God's name. God's name is holy in and of itself; it is not kept holy among us (as the Second Commandment reveals) through cursing, swearing, satanic arts, lying, and deception. Thus the First Petition is prayed as a confession of sin by those who struggle: "Above this battlefield, the First Petition must be heard since we cannot glorify God's great name out of our own reason or power, but instead we desecrate it from within ourselves."[19]

God's holy name inscribed on us in Baptism makes us Christians. God's name is hallowed when His Word is taught in truth and purity and we, His children, live holy lives in conformity to it. Luther teaches us to pray the First Petition in this way not only in the catechism but in his preaching.[20] This is also seen in the German Mass, where Luther has us pray

> *God's holy name inscribed on us in Baptism makes us Christians.*

> that God, our Father in heaven, may look with mercy on us, his
> needy children on earth, and grant us grace so that his holy name
> be hallowed by us and all the world through the pure and true
> teaching of his Word and the fervent love of our lives; that he would
> graciously turn from us all false doctrine and evil living whereby his
> precious name is being blasphemed and profaned.[21]

---

18   *Exposition of the Lord's Prayer* (1519), AE 42:33.

19   Peters, *Lord's Prayer*, 59. Also H. Thielicke: "So underneath the surface, this first petition of the Lord's Prayer is a prayer of repentance, a confession of sin of crushing weight, and none can pray who does not pass through the court of judgment, this abyss of extremity" (*Our Heavenly Father*, trans. John W. Doberstein [New York: Harper and Row, 1960], 43).

20   See, e.g., *Simple Way to Pray* (1535), AE 43:195.

21   *German Mass and Order of Service* (1526), AE 53:79.

In this way, we pray that God's name be honored among us in both doctrine and life, in word and deed. In effect, we are praying that neither our words nor our works give our Father a bad reputation.

> Just as it is a shame and a disgrace to an earthly father to have a bad, unruly child who antagonizes him in word and deed, with the result that on his account the father ends up suffering scorn and reproach, so God is dishonored if we who are called by his name and enjoy his manifold blessings fail to teach, speak, and live as upright and heavenly children, with the result that he must hear us called not children of God but children of the devil.[22]

In his explanation of the First Petition, Luther cannot help but break into supplication himself. Luther the catechist becomes Luther the man of prayer, pleading with God that He would help us teach His Word in truth and purity and lead holy lives according to it, and that He would protect us from profaning God's holy name by false teaching or a way of life contrary to God's Word. This prayer is echoed in Luther's catechism hymn:

> **Your name be hallowed. Help us, Lord,**
> **In purity to keep Your Word,**
> **That to the glory of Your name**
> **We walk before You free from blame.**
> **Let no false teaching us pervert;**
> **All poor deluded souls convert.** (*LSB* 766:2)

—∘C⁄⊃∘—

The Second Petition
Thy kingdom come.

Your kingdom come.

What does this mean?
The kingdom of God certainly comes by itself without our prayer, but we pray in this petition that it may come to us also.

---

22   LC III 44; K-W 445.

How does God's kingdom come?
God's kingdom comes when our heavenly Father gives us His
Holy Spirit, so that by His grace we believe His holy Word
and lead godly lives here in time and there in eternity.

**Merciful Father, Your kingdom comes by itself without prayers, but we
implore You to let it come to us also. Give us Your Holy Spirit, heavenly Father,
that by Your grace we believe Your Word and lead godly lives here in time and
hereafter in eternity; through Jesus Christ, Your Son, who lives and reigns with
You and the Holy Spirit, ever one God. Amen.**

That God's kingdom comes by itself and without the aid of our praying can be
seen from the Second Article, where the kingdom is described as the outcome of
Christ's death and resurrection. It is on account of His redeeming work—wherein
He purchased and won me from all sins, from death, and from the power of the
devil—that I am His own. Jesus' work locates me in His kingdom, where I live
under His gracious reign, serving Him not in servile obedience but as an heir of
everlasting righteousness, innocence, and blessedness. It is a profound paradox,
as Werner Elert puts it: "In the struggle against sin God establishes a kingdom of
sinners."[23] Christ is crucified for sinners in order that He might rule over them in
forgiveness and mercy. So in the Large Catechism, Luther answers the question
"What is the kingdom of God?" like this:

> Simply what we heard and learned above in the Creed, namely, that
> God sent his Son, Christ, our Lord, into the world to redeem and
> deliver us from the power of the devil, to bring us to himself, and
> to rule us as a king of righteousness, life, and salvation against sin,
> death, and an evil conscience. To this end he also gave us his Holy
> Spirit to deliver this to us through his holy Word and to enlighten
> and strengthen us in faith by his power.[24]

This theme is expressed in Luther's hymn:

23   Werner Elert, *The Structure of Lutheranism*, trans. Walter A. Hansen (St. Louis: Concordia, 1962),
495.

24   LC III 51; K-W 446. For more on Luther's understanding of the kingdom of God, see Elert, "The
Kingdom of Christ," in *Structure of Lutheranism*, 491–507.

> **Your kingdom come. Guard Your domain**
> **And Your eternal righteous reign.**
> **The Holy Ghost enrich our day**
> **With gifts attendant on our way.**
> **Break Satan's pow'r, defeat his rage;**
> **Preserve Your Church from age to age.** (*LSB* 766:3)

Luther points out that there is a double aspect to the coming of God's kingdom. It comes now in time when our heavenly Father gives us His Spirit so that through the Gospel we are brought to faith and live godly lives. Now in time this kingdom is hidden in the conscience of the forgiven sinner. In the words of Wolfgang Trillhaas: "Through the gospel and the gifts of the Holy Spirit, the exalted Lord carries out his reign even though his kingdom remains invisible in the present age."[25]

The kingdom will come at the end when time is fulfilled in eternity: "God's rule reaches toward us through the preaching of the Gospel and the Spirit-given obedience of faith. In this the final revelation of the Kingdom is already initiated, which culminates in Christ's return."[26] We pray as those who are already possessed by this kingdom, sons of the kingdom, and yet we await and cry out for this kingdom to come finally and decisively so that the promises of the Book of Revelation are forever fulfilled. The scope of the Second Petition embraces both the present and the future. In both aspects the focus is on the fact that the kingdom is Christ's.

> Luther places the emphasis on the office and work of God's Spirit, not on the organization of the human community. At the same time of course Luther looks at that which the Spirit does here and now on earth among us men. He underscores that particular breaking-in of God's kingdom into the satanic realm that is accomplished in Jesus' cross and resurrection and that in the working of the Holy Spirit is continually renewed. In this event, God's royal rule is already begun. Its eschatological revelation will therefore bring nothing fundamentally new. It will rather cap off the already decided battle through the final overthrow of the enemy.[27]

---

25   Wolfgang Trillhaas, "*Regnum Christi*: On the History of the Concept in Protestantism," *Lutheran World* 14 (1967): 45.

26   Peters, *Lord's Prayer*, 79.

27   Peters, *Lord's Prayer*, 81. Also note the Large Catechism: " 'The coming of God's kingdom to us' takes place in two ways: first, it comes here, in time, through the Word and faith, and second, in eternity, it

In light of this twofold coming, Luther demonstrates how we pray this petition by including this prayer in the Large Catechism:

> Dear Father, we ask you first to give us your Word, so that the gospel may be properly preached throughout the world and then that it may also be received in faith and may work and dwell in us, so that your kingdom may pervade among us through the Word and the power of the Holy Spirit and the devil's kingdom may be destroyed so that he may have no right or power over us until finally his kingdom is utterly eradicated and sin, death, and hell wiped out, that we may live forever in perfect righteousness and blessedness.[28]

No wonder that Luther then quickly adds that "we are not asking here for crumbs."[29] This petition is expansive, for all that Christ Jesus has acquired and promised is included in His kingdom. Luther piles up the adjectives to describe this kingdom in the Large Catechism: it is eternal, priceless, and inexhaustible. We are but needy beggars who are promised everything by a good and gracious Lord.

❦

The Third Petition
Thy will be done on earth as it is in heaven.

Your will be done on earth as in heaven.

What does this mean?
The good and gracious will of God is done even
without our prayer, but we pray in this petition
that it may be done among us also.

How is God's will done?
God's will is done

when He breaks and hinders every evil plan and purpose of
the devil, the world, and our sinful nature, which do not
want us to hallow God's name or let His kingdom come;

---

comes through the final revelation" (LC III 53; K-W 447).

28   LC III 54; K-W 447.

29   LC III 55; K-W 447.

and when He strengthens and keeps us firm
in His Word and faith until we die.

This is His good and gracious will.

**Blessed God, Your good and gracious will is done even without prayer, but
we pray that it may be done among us also. To that end, we petition You, holy
Lord, to break and hinder every evil plan and purpose of the devil, the world,
and our sinful nature, which do not want us to hallow Your name or let Your
kingdom come. Strengthen and keep us firm in Your Word and faith until we
die, and so fulfill in us Your good and gracious will; through Jesus Christ, our
Lord. Amen.**

We do not pray to know God's will as though we were agnostics who do not
know what the will of God is. Luther identifies God's will as good and gracious.
God's will is that sinners be turned from their unbelief and live by faith in His
Son. In short, God's will is the sinner's salvation. Under the second question
included in Luther's explanation, he gives a succinct definition of God's will in
both its negative and positive dimensions. Negatively, God's will is done in His
alien work as He breaks and hinders the schemes of the devil, the powers of the
world, and the drives of sinful flesh—all of which actively oppose God's will as
they despise His name and resist His kingdom. Luther's own prayer, included in
the Large Catechism, captures the negative aspect of the petition:

> Dear Father, your will be done and not the will of the devil or of our
> enemies, nor of those who would persecute and sup-
> press your holy Word or prevent your kingdom from
> coming; and grant that we may bear patiently and
> overcome whatever we must suffer on its account,
> so that our poor flesh may not yield or fall away through weakness
> or sloth.[30]

*God's will is the sinner's
salvation.*

Luther understands this petition as a battle cry against God's enemies. To
pray "Thy will be done" is to enter the fray.[31]

---

30 LC III 67; K-W 449.

31 Here recall the words of Walther von Loewenich: "Prayer is not a little garden of Paradise, where

Positively, God's will is done when He strengthens us and keeps us firm in His Word and faith to the end of our earthly life. In short, Luther says, "This is His good and gracious will." God's will is that His name be hallowed and His kingdom come. The hallowing of God's name and the coming of His kingdom are tied to His Word and faith. The previous two petitions are tied together with the Third Petition.

We learn to pray this petition from Jesus Himself, who prayed in that nocturnal episode in Gethsemane: "My Father, if this cannot pass unless I drink it, Your will be done" (Matthew 26:42). And we learn that the doing of God's will involves the cross and suffering. This aspect is especially accented in the Large Catechism, and it is completely consistent with the reformer's understanding of the necessity of the cross in the Christian life. Here, as well as on other occasions, Luther observes that where God's Word is preached and believed, there the holy cross will also be present: "For where God's Word is preached, accepted, or believed, and bears fruit, there the holy and precious cross will also not be far behind."[32] The cross is not a foreign element in the life of the Christian. Albrecht Peters captures Luther's point:

> Only and exclusively out of the promise of the Gospel, which overcomes the accusations of the Law, grows the faith worked by the Spirit. Where this confidence pulses through our heart and makes our conscience glad, there we cannot be silent. The new confidence of faith must break forth in word and deed, in the unfeigned service of love and free confession of the Good News so that Christ's kingdom may grow among us. Where this succeeds, there immediately the satanic reaction force appears; the "holy cross" arises as the persistent sign of the true people of God.[33]

---

the one who is weary of the Word of the cross might take a little rest, but prayer is just the battleground where the sign of the cross has been raised" (*Luther's Theology of the Cross*, trans. Herbert J. A. Bouman [Minneapolis: Augsburg, 1976], 143).

32 LC III 65; K-W 448–49. Also see Luther's 1539 treatise *On the Councils and the Church*, where Luther locates the holy cross among the marks of the Church: "The holy Christian people are externally recognized by the holy possession of the sacred cross" (AE 41:164). Also see *Sermon on Cross and Suffering* (1530), AE 51:195–208. Here Luther asserts that the Christian never seeks his own cross, but the cross will indeed come, for "each one must bear a part of the holy cross" (AE 51:198). Also see *That a Christian Should Bear His Cross* (1530), AE 43:179–86, where Luther says: "Because the devil, a mighty, evil, deceitful spirit, hates the children of God. For them the holy cross serves for learning the faith, for [learning] the power of the word, and for subduing whatever sin and pride remain. Indeed, a Christian can no more do without the cross than without food and drink" (AE 43:184).

33 Peters, *Lord's Prayer*, 108. Peters's entire section "The 'Dear Holy Cross' as Experiencing the Con-

Suffering and the cross do not stand in contradiction to the Word and faith. But they will, in various ways and times, appear in the life of the Christian, pressing the believer to reliance on God's promises and causing us to pray: "Thy will be done."

In short, this petition teaches us how to pray with steadfastness and perseverance, willing to let go of all that we have as long as God's kingdom remains. "Now this grieves our flesh and the old creature, for it means that we must remain steadfast, suffer patiently whatever befalls us, and let go whatever is taken from us."[34] Amid these reverses and losses the Christian prays the Third Petition in the confidence of the truth expressed in Luther's hymn "A Mighty Fortress Is Our God," where we sing: "The Kingdom ours remaineth" (*LSB* 656:4). The Father's good and gracious will is done in Christ, and it is for us and our salvation.

⟞∘⧼⧽∘⟝

The Fourth Petition
Give us this day our daily bread.

Give us today our daily bread.

What does this mean?
God certainly gives daily bread to everyone without
our prayers, even to all evil people, but we pray in this
petition that God would lead us to realize this and
to receive our daily bread with thanksgiving.

What is meant by daily bread?
Daily bread includes everything that has to do with the support
and needs of the body, such as food, drink, clothing, shoes,
house, home, land, animals, money, goods, a devout husband or
wife, devout children, devout workers, devout and faithful rulers,
good government, good weather, peace, health, self-control,
good reputation, good friends, faithful neighbors, and the like.

⟞⟋⟍⟝

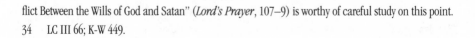

flict Between the Wills of God and Satan" (*Lord's Prayer*, 107–9) is worthy of careful study on this point.
34   LC III 66; K-W 449.

Generous Father, You certainly open Your hand to give daily bread to everyone without our prayers, even to all evil people. We pray that You would lead us to realize this and so receive our daily bread with thanksgiving, recognizing that in Your bountiful goodness You daily and richly supply everything that has to do with the support and needs of our bodies; through Jesus Christ, our Lord. Amen.

This petition directs us to the "breadbasket,"[35] as Luther says in the Large Catechism; that is, it has to do with the things needed to support and sustain creaturely life. The earthly gifts confessed in the First Article are prayed for in this petition even as believers acknowledge that God's generosity is not dependent on our prayers and that it extends to all of humanity, including unbelievers who neither confess the Creator nor look to Him for any good, much less do they give Him thanks. Jesus' words from Matthew 5:45 concerning how the Father causes His rain and sunshine to fall on the fields of both the good and evil are clearly echoed by Luther.

> God's almighty and supremely good, creative hand is stretched out over evil and good alike without our asking it. God's activity in His secular government is "on the plain" whether people now recognize and acknowledge this or not, completely analogously to the reality that also in the spiritual government, His kingdom of grace comes without our prayer and His salvific will occurs without our asking. In this petition for bread, we nevertheless ask that God would show Himself to us in His earthly goods and gifts as our benevolent Creator and merciful Savior; it is fundamentally true: Only there, where God's name is glorified, His kingdom comes to us, and His good, salutary will prevails over us, is the Creation in Christ also given to us anew so that we no longer must fear the angry judge over it, but instead may recognize the blessing Father and may be privileged to worship Him.[36]

Only in and through God's Son can we receive the Father's creaturely gifts with thanksgiving in keeping with Paul's words: "For everything created by God is good, and nothing is to be rejected if it is received with thanksgiving, for it is made holy by the word of God and prayer" (1 Timothy 4:4–5).

---

35 LC III 71; K-W 449.

36 Peters, *Lord's Prayer*, 139–40.

Luther does not spiritualize daily bread in the catechisms.

> At no point in Luther's later interpretation of "daily bread" did he
> call Jesus our daily bread, link this petition to the Lord's Supper,
> or give any "spiritual" interpretation of this petition. Instead, the
> interpretation of "daily bread" now focused completely on what one
> needs for the temporal or physical life, and especially stressed the
> role of good government and peace.[37]

Luther's treatment of "daily bread" is comprehensive because it includes
everything needed for this bodily life. None of the things included in Luther's
extended catalog—food, drink, clothing, property, animals, health, climate, and
government, to name just a few of the items Luther included—are too mundane
for spiritual prayer. Nor is it a sign of unchristian anxiety to ask for them. In fact,
faith looks to God for every good.

All people receive these gifts, but it is only believers who acknowledge God
as the donor. The Fourth Petition is actually about thanksgiving because we pray
that God would lead us to recognize that He is the Giver and that we would
receive His provisions accordingly.

> Thus, you see, God wishes to show us how he cares for us in all our
> needs and faithfully provides for our daily sustenance. Although he
> gives and provides these blessings bountifully, even to the godless
> and rogues, yet he wishes us to ask for them so that we may realize
> that we have received them from his hand and may recognize in
> them his fatherly goodness toward us. When he withdraws his hand,
> nothing can prosper or last for any length of time, as indeed we see
> and experience every day.[38]

Luther gives this petition doxological shape in his hymnic form of the Lord's Prayer:

> **Give us this day our daily bread,**
> **And let us all be clothed and fed.**
> **Save us from hardship, war, and strife;**
> **In plague and famine, spare our life,**
> **That we in honest peace may live,**
> **To care and greed no entrance give.** (*LSB* 766:5)

---

37   Kim Truebenbach, "Luther's Two Kingdoms in the Third and Fourth Petitions," *Lutheran Quarterly* 24, no. 4 (Winter 2010): 471.

38   LC III 82–83; K-W 451–52.

Praying the Fourth Petition is no substitute for work. Here the reformer's *Exposition of Psalm 127, for the Christians at Riga in Livonia* is instructive. Luther reminds his readers that "God wills that man should work, and without work He will give him nothing. Conversely, God will not give him anything because of his labor, but solely out of His own goodness and blessing."[39] It is not that work is the source of what we have; rather, Luther says "our labor is nothing other than the finding and collecting of God's gifts" that He has hidden in the world.[40] We can work without worry, for underneath our work is the work of the Creator Himself: "Indeed, one could very well say that the course of the world, and especially the doing of his saints, are God's mask, under which he conceals himself and so marvelously exercises dominion and introduces disorder in the world."[41]

The devil, of course, seeks to disrupt our reception of God's gifts. Even as the old evil foe does not want God's name to be hallowed, His kingdom to come, or His will to be done on earth, so he is ever attempting to deprive us of daily bread. Luther sees this petition as prayed against the deprivations worked by the malevolent will of Satan:

Praying the Fourth Petition is no substitute for work.

> But especially is the petition directed against our chief enemy, the devil, whose whole purpose and desire it is to take away or interfere with all we have received from God. He is not satisfied to obstruct and overthrow the spiritual order, by deceiving souls with his lies and bringing them under his power, but he also prevents and impedes the establishment of any kind of government or honorable and peaceful relations on earth. This is why he causes so much contention, murder, sedition, and war, why he sends storms and hail to destroy crops and cattle, why he poisons the air, etc. In short, it pains him that anyone should receive even a mouthful of bread from God and eat it in peace. If it were in his power and our prayer to God did not restrain him, surely we would not have a straw in the field, a penny in the house, or even an hour more of life—especially those of us who have the Word of God and would like to be Christians.[42]

---

39 *Exposition of Psalm 127* (1524), AE 45:326.
40 *Exposition of Psalm 127* (1524), AE 45:327.
41 *Exposition of Psalm 127* (1524), AE 45: 331.
42 LC III 80–81; K-W 451.

Luther sees it as urgent that Christians persevere in rubbing this petition into God's ears, as Satan never becomes slack in his murderous attempts to cause chaos in creation and drive fragile human beings to despair of God's goodness.

The Fifth Petition
And forgive us our trespasses as we forgive
those who trespass against us.

Forgive us our sins as we forgive those who sin against us.

What does this mean?
We pray in this petition that our Father in heaven would
not look at our sins, or deny our prayer because of them.
We are neither worthy of the things for which we pray,
nor have we deserved them, but we ask that He would give
them all to us by grace, for we daily sin much and surely
deserve nothing but punishment. So we too will sincerely
forgive and gladly do good to those who sin against us.

Father in heaven, do not look upon our sins or deny our prayers on account of them. We are neither worthy of the things for which we pray, nor have we deserved them, but we ask that You would give them to us by grace, for we daily sin much and deserve nothing but punishment. So we, too, will sincerely forgive and gladly do good to those who sin against us. In Your mercy, hear us, for the sake of Jesus Christ, our Savior. Amen.

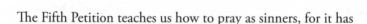

The Fifth Petition teaches us how to pray as sinners, for it has

> to do with our poor, miserable life. Although we have God's Word
> and believe, although we obey and submit to his will and are nour-
> ished by God's gift and blessing, nevertheless we are not without sin.
> We still stumble daily and transgress because we live in the world
> among people who sorely vex us and give us occasion for impatience,
> anger, vengeance, etc. Besides, the devil is after us, besieging us on
> every side and, as we have heard, directing his attacks against all the

previous petitions, so that it is not possible always to stand firm in this ceaseless conflict.[43]

Our consciences are restless, tormented by the knowledge of sin with which we are well acquainted and caught off guard by the way in which temptations to revenge flare up when we remember those whose sin has brought us suffering and loss. It is a sinful world in which we live. We sin and we are sinned against.

We are not without sin, and our prayers falter on that account. Refusing to forgive those who sin against us robs our conscience of the certainty that the Father hears our prayers. The Fifth Petition embodies the truth that the forgiveness of sins is not a onetime event; it is the continuing reality in which the Christian lives and moves and has his being.[44] Reconciled to God through the blood of Christ we cannot but forgive our fellow sinners. To refuse to do so is to spurn the forgiveness you have received from the one who made Himself the friend of sinners.

> Only because God reconciled the world to Himself in Jesus Christ can we therefore who are born of dust, as we all are caught in Adam's choking guilt, pray with joyful hearts: Father, forgive! Only because God in Jesus Christ picks us up out of the prison of selfishness and misanthropy, so that already here on earth we can forgive our human brothers and even in this way embrace in believing confidence God's forgiveness in Christ.[45]

We cannot live without the forgiveness of sins. Forgiveness is far more than a mere amnesty that erases the past and opens the path for the future. For the Scriptures and for Luther, forgiveness of sins is the necessary condition for the Christian life; it is the oxygen we breathe. Forgiveness of sins is not the gateway to the sanctified life; it is the sanctified life. Forgiveness of sins is not the stepping-stone to life and salvation. There is no life and salvation apart from the forgiveness of sins. So the prayer for forgiveness is part of the Christian's daily supplication. "For where the heart is not right with God and cannot generate such

---

43   LC III 86–87; K-W 452.

44   Note Albrecht Peters's observation: "That God does not let His prior forgiveness be limited to the onetime act of Baptism, but rather that He sets our baptism with all its power for salvation over our whole life and desires to remain active in it, is with such penetrating clarity not recognized before Luther and attested to; no exegete before him had in this petition so penetratingly pointed to God's continual forgiveness" (*Lord's Prayer*, 160–61).

45   Peters, *Lord's Prayer*, 170.

confidence, it will never dare to pray. But such a confident and joyful heart can never come except when one knows that his or her sins are forgiven."[46]

Forgiven by Christ, we forgive those who sin against us. Luther sees the fact that forgiven sinners forgive those who sin against them as a comforting sign that Christ has attached to this petition an outward sign that strengthens us to prayer with a glad conscience:

Forgiven by Christ, we forgive those who sin against us.

Dear Father, I come to you and pray that you will forgive me for this reason: not because I can make satisfaction or deserve anything by my works, but because you have promised and have set this seal on it, making it as certain as if I had received an absolution pronounced by you yourself.[47]

The Sixth Petition
And lead us not into temptation.

Lead us not into temptation.

What does this mean?
God tempts no one. We pray in this petition that God
would guard and keep us so that the devil, the world,
and our sinful nature may not deceive us or mislead us
into false belief, despair, and other great shame and vice.
Although we are attacked by these things, we pray that
we may finally overcome them and win the victory.

God, You tempt no one to sin, so we pray that You would guard and keep us so that the devil, the world, and our own sinful nature may not deceive us or mislead us into false belief, despair, and other great shame and vice. Although we are attacked by these things, we pray that, trusting in You alone, we may finally overcome them and win the victory; through Jesus Christ, our Lord. Amen.

---

46   LC III 92; K-W 453.
47   LC III 97; K-W 453.

Temptation has as its target the First Commandment, so Luther reminds us that the world, the flesh, and the devil are the causes of temptation, not God. Temptation aims to divorce believers from God, to tear them away from the God who loves them so that they no longer fear, love, and trust in Him above all things. No Christian is exempt from temptation; the Lord Christ Himself was tempted yet remained without sin. That is why Luther says we are given this petition to pray:

> Every Christian must endure such great, grievous perils and attacks— grievous enough even if they come one at a time. As long as we remain in this vile life, where we are attacked, hunted, and harried on all sides, we are constrained to cry out and pray every hour that God may not allow us to become faint and weary and to fall back into sin, shame, and unbelief. Otherwise it is impossible to overcome even the smallest attack.[48]

The Sixth Petition is prayed under the pressure of assaults that are too great to be overcome by our own energy or strength.

Temptation comes, Luther says, from three sources: the devil, the world, and our sinful nature.[49] These powers seek to overthrow the redemption accomplished by Jesus Christ. In the Large Catechism, Luther examines the dynamics of each. The devil "baits and badgers us on all sides,"[50] tormenting the conscience.

> His purpose is to make us scorn and despise both the Word and the works of God, to tear us away from faith, hope, and love, to draw us into unbelief, false security, and stubbornness, or, on the contrary, to drive us into despair, denial of God, blasphemy, and countless other abominable sins.[51]

Terrifying the conscience with his incessant attacks, Satan calls into question God's truthfulness and reliability and seeks to set the conscience into opposition to God, from which it cannot but fall into despair. Despair is the necessary fruit of unbelief and misbelief.

---

48   LC III 105; K-W 454.

49   "The triad of sin, the world, and the devil . . . was often combined as early as in medieval catechetics, from which Luther appropriated it for his own explanations to the catechism" (Bernhard Lohse, *Martin Luther's Theology: Its Historical and Systematic Development*, trans. Roy A. Harrisville [Minneapolis: Fortress, 1999], 253).

50   LC III 104; K-W 454.

51   LC III 104; K-W 454.

The world with its vaunted but vacant promises is also a source of temptation. These Luther identifies as enticements to a worldliness that would find satisfaction in creaturely comfort and prestige as well as rejoicing in violence and injustice to achieve one's own place of privilege. This temptation, Luther says, "drives us to anger and impatience . . . perfidy, vengeance, cursing, reviling, slander, arrogance, and pride, along with fondness for luxury, honor, fame, and power."[52] Here the temptation is to exchange the worship of the Creator for carnal security in things that are elusive and temporal. It is "the desires of the eyes and pride in possessions" of which the apostle speaks in 1 John 2:16.

Luther rounds out the unholy triad with "our sinful nature" or the "flesh."[53] Our sinful nature is "the old creature around our necks" until our death. It is only in death that this old Adam will be once and for all time divorced from the new man. Then only the new man will remain and live with Christ. In the meantime, we continue to pray as those who are pulled and pushed by the lusts of the old nature, by such things as sexual immorality, drunkenness, gluttony, laziness, and deception, to list some of the items Luther includes in his treatment of this petition in the Large Catechism.

Given the cunning and force of these enemies, Luther realizes that the Christian is constantly imperiled and under attack. According to their age or station in life, Christians might experience temptation differently. For example, Luther sees youth as particularly prone to fleshly temptation, while older adults often are more susceptible to worldly temptations. Those in positions of spiritual authority, Luther believes, are most likely to be tempted by the devil. All Christians, in one way or another, will experience temptation. Whether weak or strong in the faith, all Christians are endangered by temptation. Thus Luther urges constant and watchful prayer:

> All Christians, in one way or another, will experience temptation.

> Accordingly we Christians must be armed and expect every day to be under continuous attack. Then we will not go about securely and heedlessly as if the devil were far from us, but will at all times expect his blows and fend them off. Even if at present I am chaste, patient,

---

52   LC III 103; K-W 454.

53   Udo Schnelle describes *sarx* ("flesh") in the Pauline writings as "an alien power that attempts to take it [the person] over as its own domain" (*Theology of the New Testament*, trans. M. Eugene Boring [Grand Rapids: Baker Academic, 2009], 284). Schnelle also notes that those who live in "the realm of the flesh [are] those who live out of their own resources and trust in themselves" (*Apostle Paul: His Life and Theology*, trans. M. Eugene Boring [Grand Rapids: Baker Academic, 2005], 498). Schnelle's description confirms Luther's understanding.

kind, and firm in the faith, the devil is likely at this very hour to send such an arrow into my heart that I can scarcely endure, for he is an enemy who never lets up or becomes weary; when one attack ceases, new ones always arise.[54]

Only "prayer can resist him and drive him back."[55]

The victory will not be accomplished by the skill of the Christian's struggle but by the promises of Christ in which we stand, particularly the promise of the Comforter (see John 14:25–27; 16:7–11). Luther gives succinct expression to this truth not only in the catechisms but also in his hymn:

> **Lead not into temptation, Lord,**
> **Where our grim foe and all his horde**
> **Would vex our souls on ev'ry hand.**
> **Help us resist, help us to stand**
> **Firm in the faith, a mighty host,**
> **Through comfort of the Holy Ghost.** (*LSB* 766:7)

The Seventh Petition
But deliver us from evil.

But deliver us from evil.

What does this mean?
We pray in this petition, in summary, that our Father in heaven would rescue us from every evil of body and soul, possessions and reputation, and finally, when our last hour comes, give us a blessed end, and graciously take us from this valley of sorrow to Himself in heaven.

Our Father in heaven, rescue us from every evil of body and soul, possessions and reputation, and finally, when our last hour comes, give us a blessed

---

54 LC III 109; K-W 455.
55 LC III 111; K-W 455.

end and graciously take us from this valley of sorrows to Yourself in heaven; through Jesus Christ, our Lord. Amen.

The Seventh Petition summarizes all that has been requested in the Lord's Prayer. Like the other petitions, it is pointedly and aggressively aimed against the devil, who is a liar and murderer from the beginning (John 8:44). "He ultimately stands behind the diversity of evil. Against him all the individual petitions of the Lord's Prayer are directed."[56] This petition embraces the evil—whether spiritual or physical—that may happen to us in this life, as demonstrated by Luther's use of the phrase "every evil of body and soul, possessions and reputation." It is as though Luther were pulling into summation everything confessed of the Ten Commandments, Creed, and first six petitions of the Lord's Prayer. Although the devil's might is real, Christians are equipped to pray against the evil one with boldness and confidence, in a good conscience, as those who are children of the Father in heaven.

Luther is both graphic and biblical in his depiction of Satan's potency and the reach of his infernal domain:

> This petition includes all the evil that may befall us under the devil's kingdom: poverty, disgrace, death, and, in short, all the tragic misery and heartache, of which there is so incalculably much on earth. For because the devil is not only a liar but a murderer as well, he incessantly seeks our life and vents his anger by causing accidents and injury to our bodies. He crushes some and drives others to insanity; some he drowns in water, and many he hounds to suicide or other dreadful catastrophes.[57]

These evils are not just banalities that happen in a broken world; Luther sees them as rooted in a malevolent and personal being identified in the Scriptures as the devil. Human beings—Christians included—are susceptible to his tactics, so we are to pray to the Father for rescue.

The rescue for which we are emboldened to pray is both temporal and eternal. The final petition of the Lord's Prayer is uttered against the eschatological horizon:

---

56   Peters, *Lord's Prayer*, 204. Note Luther's language in the Large Catechism in reference to the Greek that speaks of deliverance from the evil [one]: "It seems to be speaking of the devil as the sum of all evil in order that the entire substance of our prayer may be directed against our archenemy. . . . For if God did not support us, we would not be safe from him for single hour" (LC III 113, 116; K-W 455–56).

57   LC III 115; K-W 455.

"and finally, when our last hour comes, give us a blessed end, and graciously take us from this valley of sorrow to Himself in heaven." Werner Elert wisely noted: "Some live in the light of the Last Day, others in its shadow."[58] Christians live in its light and so pray with confident hope for the final deliverance through the darkness of death into the radiance of heaven's unfailing light.

> From evil, Lord, deliver us;
> The times and days are perilous.
> Redeem us from eternal death,
> And, when we yield our dying breath,
> Console us, grant us calm release,
> And take our souls to You in peace. (*LSB* 766:8)

The Conclusion
For Thine is the kingdom and the power and
the glory forever and ever. Amen.

For the kingdom, the power, and the glory
are Yours now and forever. Amen.

What does this mean?
This means that I should be certain that these petitions are
pleasing to our Father in heaven, and are heard by Him; for
He Himself has commanded us to pray in this way and has
promised to hear us. Amen, amen means "yes, yes, it shall be so."

Father in heaven, give us the certainty that the petitions we make according to Your command and promise are pleasing to You and are heard by You, so that with all boldness and confidence we might say: Amen, amen. Yes, yes, it shall be so; through Your Son, Jesus Christ, who has taught us to pray in this way. Amen.

---

58   Werner Elert, *Last Things*, ed. Rudolph F. Norden, trans. Martin Bertram (St. Louis: Concordia, 1974), 28.

"Amen" is the great word of faith. It is the confession that God's promises are true, reliable, and trustworthy. To pray according to God's command and promise is to call upon the Father with the certainty born of faith, that is, with all boldness and confidence that He is not deaf to our cries but hears and answers according to His good and gracious will. Sometimes learning to utter the "Amen" is the hardest part of prayer, for with this word we commit our petitions to the Father who hears us not because of our many words stacked one upon another, as though we would be heard on account of the length, sincerity, or persuasiveness of our speech, but because He is our Father. The catechism teaches us to pray on the strength of the Amen in the way of 2 Corinthians 1:20, where Paul says all the promises of God find their Yes in Christ.[59]

So Luther's explanation of the Lord's Prayer ends where it began: with faith. Luther underscores the fact that

> the efficacy of prayer consists in our learning also to say Amen to it—that is, not to doubt that our prayer is surely heard and will be answered. This word is nothing else than an unquestioning word of faith on the part of the one who does not pray as a matter of luck but knows that God does not lie because he has promised to grant it. Where there is no faith like this, there also can be no true prayer.[60]

Prayer is the voice of faith that clings to the promises of God and is bold to call upon Him on this basis. Prayer depends on the promise of Christ Jesus that gives us "the ground to nag and pester the Promisor."[61] The Father delights in such nagging and pestering when His children rub His promises into His ears with the Amen of faith.

---

59   Mark Seifrid captures the biblical significance of Luther's use of the Amen: "It is the verbal response that arises from those who have been given the gift of salvation. It is a word of faith and hope in the glory that is yet to be revealed. God's saving Yes in the crucified and risen Christ does not return to him empty but creates its own reception and thus brings the fruit of thanksgiving and praise" (*The Second Letter to the Corinthians* [Grand Rapids: Eerdmans, 2014], 63–64). Luther's "yes, yes, it shall be so" is the confident affirmation that all of the things for which we ask in the Lord's Prayer are given on account of Christ.

60   LC III 119–20; K-W 456. Also note how Luther accents faith in opposition to doubt in the paraphrase of the Lord's Prayer in *German Mass and Order of Service* (1526): "All those who earnestly desire these things will say from their very hearts: Amen, trusting without any doubt that it is Yea and answered in heaven as Christ has promised: Whatever you ask in prayer, believe that you shall receive it, and you will [Mark 11:24]" (AE 53:79).

61   Steven Paulson, *Lutheran Theology* (London: T&T Clark, 2011), 205.

The Amen links God's Word and faith in opposition to doubt. Luther echoes this in the final stanza of his catechetical hymn on the Lord's Prayer. Doubt is the opposite of faith, and as such, it is conquered only by God's Word and name. Amen is the assertion of this Word and the divine name upon which prayer stands:

> Amen, that is, so shall it be.
> Make strong our faith in You, that we
> May doubt not but with trust believe
> That what we ask we shall receive.
> Thus in Your name and at Your Word
> We say, "Amen, O hear us, Lord!" (*LSB* 766:9)

Prayer is the voice of faith that clings to the promises of God.

CHAPTER 5

Holy Baptism

Calling On the Name Given to Us

INTRODUCTION

In Baptism, the Father claims lost and condemned sinners as His own dear children for the sake of the suffering and death of His Son, and He endows them with His Holy Spirit. Baptism locates sinners under the saving lordship of Christ:

> The full extent of the eschatological effect, forgiveness of sins and new life, being delivered from the tyranny of the powers that do harm and being moved instead to be under the lordship of Christ, all such aspects are attributed to Baptism, since by means of His name, the sanctifying presence of God is at play in this action.[1]

Adopted by the Father, we are given the inheritance of sons, enabling us to call God "our Father." Baptized into His name, we now have the confidence and boldness to pray as dear children address a dear father. For Luther, Christian prayer presupposes Baptism. We call upon the name of the Lord because we have been baptized into this holy name. Baptism gives us the pledge that we are not orphans, illegitimate, or accidental offspring but true children, privileged to call the God and Father who raised Jesus from the dead our true Father.

---

1   Albrecht Peters, *Baptism and Lord's Supper*, trans. Thomas H. Trapp, Commentary on Luther's Catechisms 4 (St. Louis: Concordia, 2012), 101.

FIRST

What is baptism?
Baptism is not just plain water, but it is the water included
in God's command and combined with God's word.

Which is that word of God?
Christ our Lord says in the last chapter of Matthew:
"Therefore go and make disciples of all nations,
baptizing them in the name of the Father and of the
Son and of the Holy Spirit." (Matt. 28:19)

———

**Lord Jesus Christ, You instituted Baptism, which is not just plain water
but water included in Your command and combined with Your word when
You said, "Therefore go and make disciples of all nations, baptizing them in
the name of the Father and of the Son and of the Holy Spirit." Grant us always
to cherish our Baptism, trusting in the promises You make to us there, and so
by this gift come to receive the inheritance of eternal life; for You live and reign
with the Father and the Holy Spirit, one God, now and forever. Amen.**

The crucified and risen Lord Jesus Christ instituted and established Baptism.
Jesus is the Son of Man to whom all dominion has been given (see Daniel 7:14),
who was put to death for the sins of the world and was raised from the dead for
our justification. The Baptism that He establishes rests on His authority. In this
Baptism, Jesus extends His lordship as He makes of sinners disciples.[2] So the

---

2 Of the dominical words of Matthew 28, Edmund Schlink says: "Jesus is here speaking as the Exalted
One who has all things under His feet, as the Lord whom God has installed at His right hand. But having
been given all authority does not mean that it is already acknowledged by all. Putting all things under
Him does not yet mean that all things are obedient to Him. The world's resistance is already futile and will
one day be shattered in the Judgment. But those who acknowledge His rule and become His disciples will
be saved. It is this saving pervasion of all that has been made subject to the exalted Lord that is the concern of the baptismal command. The concern is in every respect with the whole: '*All* authority' has been
given to Jesus, '*all* nations' are to be made His disciples, '*all*' that Jesus has commanded is to be taught
and observed, and Jesus will be with His people '*all*' the days until the close of the age" (*The Doctrine of
Baptism*, trans. Herbert J. A. Bouman [St. Louis: Concordia, 1972], 9).

catechism begins not with discourse on the life-giving or cleansing properties of water, or theories of the need for rituals of initiation, or Old Testament events involving water, but with the instituting words of Jesus Christ.[3] "Baptism is not just plain water, but it is the water included in God's command and combined with God's word."

Luther never veers away from the Lord's institution of Baptism when extolling it as the "excellent, glorious, and exalted"[4] sacrament that it is. It is no mere external trapping that can be peeled away to reveal some more sublime spiritual significance.

> But no matter how external it may be, here stand God's Word and command that have instituted, established, and confirmed baptism. What God institutes and commands cannot be useless. Rather, it is a most precious thing, even though to all appearances it may not be worth a straw. . . . What is more, it is performed in his name. So the words read, "Go, baptize," not "in your name" but "in God's name."[5]

God's command, not human notions of religiosity, is the foundation for Baptism.

The command to baptize carries with it a promise. Steven Paulson says:

> The word that is put into the water is not a general word, but a specific one: a promise given to us. That word is by Christ's command: "Go therefore and make disciples of all nations, baptizing them in the name of the Father and of the Son and of the Holy Spirit" (Matt 28:19). In this word, God bestows his name by proclaiming it out loud (fulfilling the third commandment in which an unholy thing becomes holy) and so fulfilling the second commandment to keep the name holy by grasping it. The name is given so that we may call upon the Lord on the final day, just as Joel promised—a promise that Paul extended even to the Gentiles: "Everyone who calls on the name of the Lord shall be saved" (Rom 10:13; Joel 2:32).[6]

---

3   Here also see Oswald Bayer: "The sign [water] certainly belongs to it [Baptism] as well, but one cannot just meditate on water alone—possibly by reflecting on the danger it can bring, its power to cleanse and to give life—if one seeks to recognize the essence of baptism. Instead, the element is saturated through and through and comprehended in the biblical Word: based on the commission to baptize in Matthew 28 as well as the promise of baptism in Mark 16:16" (*Luther's Theology*, 265).

4   LC IV 7; K-W 457.

5   LC IV 8–9; K-W 457.

6   Steven Paulson, "Graspable God," *Word & World* 32, no. 1 (Winter 2012): 54. Used with permission. All rights reserved.

To be baptized in this name "is to be baptized not by human beings but by God himself. Although it is performed by human hands, it is nevertheless truly God's own act."[7] This gives Baptism both its permanence and certainty. Baptism is trustworthy because it is not the work of man but of the God who puts His name in it. To pray as baptized children of God is to call upon that saving name in the confidence that the Father's ears are never closed to His children.

Baptism is trustworthy because it is not the work of man but of the God who puts His name in it.

Baptism "is not merely a portal through which the Christian enters the church in order to leave that portal behind."[8] For Luther, Baptism is in the present tense. It is not so much "I was baptized" but "I am baptized." Baptized into Christ, we have access to the Father through the Spirit who has brought us to faith, and so we are enlivened to prayer.

SECOND

What benefits does Baptism give?
It works forgiveness of sins, rescues from death and the devil, and gives eternal salvation to all who believe this, as the words and promises of God declare.

Which are these words and promises of God?
Christ our Lord says in the last chapter of Mark: "Whoever believes and is baptized will be saved, but whoever does not believe will be condemned." (Mark 16:16)

Lord Jesus Christ, by Your death You have purchased and won for us forgiveness of sins, rescuing us from death and the devil and obtaining eternal salvation which You now work in Baptism. Give us Your Spirit that we may believe what You have said, "Whoever believes and is baptized will be saved," and so receive

---

7   LC IV 10; K-W 457. Also see Lennart Pinomaa: "In the baptismal rite it is God himself who acts, even though he puts on a costume of human activity" (*Faith Victorious: An Introduction to Luther's Theology*, trans. Walter J. Kukkonen [Philadelphia: Fortress, 1963], 139).

8   Werner Elert, *Structure of Lutheranism*, 296.

these gifts of forgiveness of sins, victory over death and the devil, and eternal salvation, as Your words and promises declare. Amen.

The catechism links the institution of Baptism in Matthew 28:19 to the promise of Baptism in Mark 16:16 by describing the benefits of Baptism. The gifts that Christ acquired—which we confess in Luther's explanation to the Second Article of the Creed, that He "has redeemed me, a lost and condemned person, purchased and won me from all sins, from death, and from the power of the devil; not with gold or silver, but with His holy, precious blood and with His innocent suffering and death"—are packed in Baptism ("[Baptism] works forgiveness of sins, rescues from death and the devil, and gives eternal salvation to all who believe this"). Here Luther does two things. First, he locates the benefit of Baptism in Christ's atoning death. Second, he shows that faith does not constitute Baptism, but it is only through faith that the benefits of Baptism are received. Baptism carries with it a divine promise, and the only thing to be done with a promise is to believe it, to trust it. Oswald Bayer helpfully states: "The *faith* consists in submission to what is given in the sacrament: forgiveness of sins."[9]

Baptism works for the forgiveness of sins, and as such it brings about a change of lords. Sin is no longer lord; Jesus is. Edmund Schlink nicely captures this thought:

> The forgiveness which is imparted through Baptism is determined by the fact that the baptized is assigned to the Crucified as to the living, present, and active Lord. Therefore in this forgiveness it is not simply a matter of removing a purely cultic impurity, nor of pardoning isolated transgressions of divine precepts, nor of the cancellation of a specific individual guilt. Beyond all of this the forgiveness which is imparted through Baptism is a change of dominion. Through Baptism man is removed from the dominion of sin and placed under the rule of Christ.[10]

In Baptism, sin is forgiven, and with this forgiveness there is rescue from death and the devil. Forgiveness of sins is not the first step to eternal salvation; it is

---

9   Bayer, *Luther's Theology*, 265. Also see Peters: "Baptism is not merely something instituted by God as a legal demand, but it is at the same time and primarily God's grace-filled promise, which as such is complete in itself, admittedly taken hold of by us in faith, and which is to be held onto firmly" (*Baptism and Lord's Supper*, 97).

10   Edmund Schlink, *Doctrine of Baptism*, 44–45.

eternal salvation. In Baptism, I am "His own and live under Him in His kingdom and serve Him in everlasting righteousness, innocence, and blessedness, just as He is risen from the dead, lives and reigns to all eternity."[11]

In contrast to the Roman Catholic notion that Baptism works simply by its performance (*ex opera operatio*), Luther stresses the necessity of faith that receives these gifts "as the words and promises of God declare." Faith must have something to believe in:

> Thus faith clings to the water and believes it to be baptism, in which there is sheer salvation and life, not through the water, as we have sufficiently stated, but through its incorporation with God's Word and ordinance and the joining of his name to it. When I believe this, what else is it but believing in God as the one who has bestowed and implanted his Word in baptism and has offered us this eternal thing within which we can grasp this treasure?[12]

Because Baptism is not a human work but God's work, Luther asserts that it is by faith alone that this divine work can be received. There is no contradiction between "Baptism . . . now saves you" (1 Peter 3:21) and the fact that Christians are saved by faith alone. Luther writes: "Thus you see plainly that baptism is not a work that we do but that it is a treasure that God gives us and faith grasps, just as the Lord Christ upon the cross is not a work but a treasure placed in the setting of the Word and offered to us in the Word and received by faith."[13] God established Baptism for the sake of faith.[14] Faith does not establish Baptism, but

---

11   The language of the Small Catechism is echoed in the Large Catechism: "Because we now know what baptism is and how it is to be regarded, we must also learn why and for what purpose it has been instituted, that is, what benefits, gifts, and effects it brings. Nor can we better understand this than from the words of Christ quoted above, 'The one who believes and is baptized will be saved.' This is the simplest way to put it: the power, effect, benefit, fruit, and purpose of baptism is that it saves. For no one is baptized in order to become a prince, but, as the words say, 'to be saved.' To be saved, as everyone well knows, is nothing else than to be delivered from sin, death, and the devil, to enter into Christ's kingdom, and to live with him forever" (LC IV 23–25; K-W 459).

12   LC IV 29; K-W 460.

13   LC IV 37; K-W 461. Here also see the discussion by Werner Elert, who develops the thought that Baptism gives assurance by giving believers something to hold onto amid living and dying. "Thus Baptism becomes exactly analogous to the Word, on which faith relies. But it differs from it (1) because Baptism is a concrete act, therefore the 'visible Word' (*verbum visibile*), and (2) because here the Christian is addressed by God in a wholly personal way, is called by name, and is accepted personally as a child" (*Structure of Lutheranism*, 295).

14   Faith and Baptism may not be pitted against each other. Peter Brunner rightly observes: "There can be no Spirit-worked faith in the Gospel which does not desire and lead to Baptism" ("Salvation and the

faith that God works with His Word in the water is the only way in which the benefits of Baptism are received.[15]

This theme is also accented in one of Luther's postils for Ascension Day based on Mark 16:14–20. Here Luther seeks to demonstrate that from Christ's institution of Baptism and the promise He attached to it, it is evident that He is the actor in Baptism:

> Now, it is obvious that in the words He speaks—"Teach all nations and baptize them," etc., and "Whoever believes and is baptized"— He is pointing us not to our works and the doctrine of the Law, but to His works and gift, which we cannot receive otherwise than through faith. That is the treasure through which we are saved, not earned or merited by us, but given to us by Him. We cannot ever say or boast that Christ (in whom we believe) or Baptism (which we receive on His [authority]) are our doing or were brought about by any human being.[16]

Then Luther concludes by noting that the controversy over Baptism is not about whether or not Christians are to do good works. Christians will do good works because they are a fruit of faith, but Baptism is not one of these good works:

> Rather, we are dealing with a greater matter, that is, not what we do, but where we are to seek and can surely get that through which we are saved from sin and death and have eternal life and salvation. Here Christ announces and explains exactly what the chief doctrine of the Gospel is to be; He bases it only on faith and Baptism, and He concludes that we are saved because of it, when we have Christ through faith and Baptism.[17]

Because Baptism is God's work received in faith, it is the foundation and platform upon which Christian prayer stands. The very externality of Baptism,

---

Office of the Ministry," *Lutheran Quarterly* 15, no. 2 [May 1963]: 112).

15   Here see Holsten Fagerberg: "Baptism as such is not dependent upon our faith. What God has determined and promised is not influenced by our changing attitudes. But faith is necessary if Baptism is to be received in a way that brings salvation. The strong emphasis on Baptism as a work of God—whether men recognize it as such or not—did not lead the reformers to the *opus operatum* position" (*A New Look at the Lutheran Confessions [1529–1537]*, trans. Gene J. Lund [St. Louis: Concordia, 1972], 180).

16   *Church Postil* (1540–44), sermon for Ascension on Mark 16:14–20, AE 77:278.

17   *Church Postil* (1540–44), sermon for Ascension on Mark 16:14–20, AE 77:278.

water saturated with God's Word, gives the Christian a divine promise to rub into God's ears in prayer: "I am baptized!"

THIRD

How can water do such great things?
Certainly not just water, but the word of God in and
with the water does these things, along with the faith
which trusts this word of God in the water. For without
God's word the water is plain water and no Baptism. But
with the word of God it is a Baptism, that is, a life-giving
water, rich in grace, and a washing of the new birth in the
Holy Spirit, as St. Paul says in Titus, chapter three:

"He saved us through the washing of rebirth and renewal
by the Holy Spirit, whom He poured out on us generously
through Jesus Christ our Savior, so that, having been justified
by His grace, we might become heirs having the hope of
eternal life. This is a trustworthy saying." (Titus 3:5–8)

Lord Christ, it is certainly not just water, but the Word of God in the water that does these great things, along with the faith which trusts this Word of God in the water, for without God's Word the water is plain water and no Baptism. We confess and trust that with Your Word, this water is a Baptism, that is, a life-giving water, rich in grace, and a washing of new life in the Holy Spirit, as Your apostle teaches: "He saved us through the washing of rebirth and renewal by the Holy Spirit, whom He poured out on us generously through Jesus Christ our Savior, so that, having been justified by His grace, we might become heirs having the hope of eternal life" (Titus 3:5–8). Give us hearts of faith to cling to this trustworthy saying, not doubting but firmly believing that this Baptism now saves us. Hear us, for we pray in Your name, Lord Jesus. Amen.

In this third part, Luther now draws attention to the efficacy of God's Word that is in and with the water that works regeneration. It is this Word which distinguishes the water of Baptism from all other waters:

> Baptism is a very different thing from all other water, not by virtue of the natural substance but because something nobler is added, for God himself stakes his honor, his power, and his might on it. Therefore it is not simply natural water, but a divine, heavenly, holy, and blessed water—praise it in any other terms you can—all by virtue of the Word, which is a heavenly, holy Word that no one can sufficiently extol, for it contains all that is God's.[18]

---

18 LC IV 17; K-W 458. Also note Jonathan Trigg on the coherence of water and the Word in Luther's understanding: "Luther embraces Augustine's formula, *accedat verbum ad elementum et fir sacramentum* (the Word is added to the element and makes it a sacrament) as the foundation of his understanding of baptism. Luther's emphatic insistence on the inseparability of Word and water provides him with the answer to those he sees as despising the water as mere water, such as a cow drinks or a maid cooks with (WA 51:129, 26–36; LW 51:376; BSLK 695; BC 459). Luther's understanding of the means of grace through which God chooses to reveal himself will tolerate neither the despising of the appointed externals nor an attempt to seek God apart from them. To treat the water of baptism as mere water is to ignore the Word joined to that water; it leads to an idolatrous attempt to seek God other than where he has chosen to be found, namely concealed under his opposite, hidden under and revealed in something as ordinary and unimpressive as water" ("Luther on Baptism and Penance," in *The Oxford Handbook of Martin Luther's Theology*, ed. Robert Kolb, Irene Dingel, L'ubomír Batka [Oxford: Oxford University Press, 2014], 312).

God's Word added to the water makes Baptism what it is, a holy washing of regeneration as the apostle describes it in Titus 3:5–8.[19] "Baptism is a divine water because the Word places God's name with it."[20]

The language of "rebirth and renewal" is the vocabulary of re-creation, a new genesis of which the triune God is the author.

> As the author of the new creation God now fulfills the promise, "a new heart I will give you, and a new spirit I will put within you; and I will take out of your flesh the heart of stone and will give you a heart of flesh" (Ezek. 36:26). The new creation of man in Christ through the Holy Spirit is called regeneration.[21]

Just as Adam did not cooperate with God in his creation, so his sinful descendants cannot participate in their own regeneration. Dead in sin, they cannot bring themselves to life. "In no way can man recreate and renew himself or give himself a new birth. The more he tries to free himself of himself the more he falls back upon himself."[22]

---

19   In his lectures on Titus given in 1527 (two years prior to preparing the catechism), Luther speaks against the sectarians who despise Baptism on the grounds that it is mere water: "Beware of their madness, because when an outward thing is grasped through the Word of God, it is a saving thing. If the humanity of Christ were without the Word, it would be a vain thing. But now we are saved through His blood and His body, because the Word is joined to it. Thus Baptism bears the Word of God by which the water is sanctified, and we are sanctified in the water" (*Lectures on Titus*, AE 29:82). Also note Luther on John 3:4, where he speaks of the water of Baptism as a Spirit-filled water: "Here Christ also speaks of the Holy Spirit and teaches us to regard Baptism as spiritual, yes, a Spirit-filled water, in which the Holy Spirit is present and active; in fact, the entire Holy Trinity is there. . . . But after the Holy Spirit is added to it, we have more than mere water. It becomes a veritable bath of rejuvenation, a living bath which washes and purges man of sin and death, which cleanses him of all sin" (*Sermons on John 1–2* [1538–40/1847], AE 22:283–84). Here also see Hermann Sasse: "Baptism is 'the washing of regeneration and renewal in the Holy Spirit.' In Baptism the Holy Spirit is bestowed; we are 'baptized into one body' (1 Cor. 12:13). According to Rom. 6:3, the baptized are baptized into Christ's death. Those are all realities that happen not alongside of Baptism but in it. Water Baptism in the New Testament, as long as it is Baptism into Christ, in the name of Christ, is Spirit Baptism; it is being born anew and at the same time from above 'of water *and* the Spirit' (John 3:5). The New Testament knows nothing of a being born again without Baptism or apart from Baptism. Baptism is therefore not a sign but a means of regeneration" ("Holy Baptism," trans. Norman Nagel, in vol. 1 of *Letters to Lutheran Pastors*, ed. Matthew C. Harrison [St. Louis: Concordia, 2013], 60).

20   Robert Kolb, "What Benefit Does the Soul Receive from a Handful of Water? Luther's Preaching on Baptism, 1528–1539," in *Luther's Way of Thinking: Introductory Essays* (Trivandrum, India: Luther Academy India, 2006), 113.

21   Schlink, *Doctrine of Baptism*, 82.

22   Schlink, *Doctrine of Baptism*, 82.

Baptism is the sacrament of justification. Luther actually remarks in *Babylonian Captivity of the Church* that Baptism is "full and complete justification."[23] Baptism is our righteousness. In it our sins are forgiven, and we are saved through the washing of rebirth and renewal by the Holy Spirit to live as those who have the hope of eternal life. Paul calls this a "trustworthy" saying (Titus 3:8). Baptism gives us the assurance that the Spirit has made us children of the Father through Christ Jesus, and with that we have courage and boldness to pray.

FOURTH

What does such baptizing with water indicate?
It indicates that the Old Adam in us should by daily contrition and repentance be drowned and die with all sins and evil desires, and that a new man should daily emerge and arise to live before God in righteousness and purity forever.

Where is this written?
St. Paul writes in Romans chapter six: "We were therefore buried with Him through baptism into death in order that, just as Christ was raised from the dead through the glory of the Father, we too may live a new life." (Rom. 6:4)

Lord God, You have taught us through Your holy apostle: "We were therefore buried with Him through baptism into death in order that, just as Christ was raised from the dead through the glory of the Father, we too may live a new life" (Romans 6:4). Cause the old Adam in us to be drowned by daily contrition and repentance with all sins and evil desires, so that a new man might daily emerge and arise to live before You in righteousness and purity forever; through Jesus Christ, our Lord. Amen.

In the fourth part, Luther comes to the significance of Baptism for the ongoing life of the Christian. For Luther, the language of death and life is the language of

---

23   *Babylonian Captivity* (1520), AE 36:67.

Baptism. For Luther, this is not an "allegory" but a real and "joyous exchange" (*froeliche Wechsel*):

> Baptism is not a metaphor or image used by the church for some other purpose than forgiveness of sin. It is an act that gives Christ's promise to a sinner who needs forgiveness. Baptism forgives by killing and making alive through the word proclaimed to sinners. It kills not metaphorically but really. It does not kill only my lower parts, letting me preserve my *imago dei*. It kills all of me, even the highest parts. It gives then the Holy Spirit, who creates us anew, giving new life. That life trusts Christ and his righteousness, not one's own righteousness, and so finds itself pleasing to God on account of Christ. We can conclude, therefore, that baptism equals justification.[24]

The significance of Baptism is found in the rhythm of Christian life: dying and rising as described by Paul in Romans 6:1–11. Prompted by the apostle's words, Luther writes:

> Thus a Christian life is nothing else than a daily baptism, begun once and continuing ever after. For we must keep at it without ceasing, always purging whatever pertains to the old Adam, so that whatever belongs to the new creature may come forth. What is the old creature? It is what is born in us from Adam, irascible, spiteful, envious, unchaste, greedy, lazy, proud—yes—and unbelieving; it is beset with all vices and by nature has nothing good in it. Now, when we enter Christ's kingdom, this corruption must daily decrease so that the longer we live the more gentle, patient, and meek we become, and the more we break away from greed, hatred, envy, and pride.[25]

Baptism is lethal; it is death to sin. It puts an end to the old creature born from Adam who has inherited from him all of his God-defying characteristics. Paulson rightly notes that "baptism is not a human act of obedience to a law, it is God's attack on sin by attacking the actual sinner; it is death."[26] But the outcome of this

---

24 Paulson, "Graspable God," 55.

25 LC IV 65–67, K-W 465. Oswald Bayer: "The fourth baptismal question in the Small Catechism proves that Luther did not think of baptism as an isolated act, but that it decidedly includes the *Christian life* that proceeds from it as well" (*Luther's Theology*, 267, *emphasis original*).

26 Paulson, *Lutheran Theology*, 155.

death is life, for in the baptismal death we are united with Christ's death so that, just as He was raised from the dead, we, too, may live a new live (Romans 6:4).

As we have already observed, Luther does not see Baptism as the first point in a sacramental spectrum or as a mere rite of initiation, but it is the act of the triune God that embraces the totality of the Christian's life. Baptism is, as we have said, "present tense." Baptism remains a constant for the Christian as he or she lives in repentance and faith, dying to sin and living in Christ. As Oswald Bayer says, "A Christian believer never develops beyond baptism, as long as he or she lives, no matter how much one has grown, no matter how much one has learned, and no matter what changes one has experienced."[27] Only in our own bodily death will we be finished with Baptism as it will be fulfilled once and for all in a resurrection where death will forever be in the past.

In unbelief one may jump overboard and perish, but the ship of Baptism is unsinkable.

In the meantime, the Christian does not move beyond Baptism to some other project, such as penance. Luther was critical of Jerome's imagery of penance as a plank that the Christian may grab onto for a chance at life once the ship of Baptism is shipwrecked by the hurricane of sin.[28] In unbelief one may jump overboard and perish, but the ship of Baptism is unsinkable. Repentance is a return to one's Baptism, clinging by faith to what God has promised there: the forgiveness of sins, deliverance from death and the devil, and eternal salvation. Jonathan Trigg says, "Progress in the Christian life can never be progress away from the beginning of baptism, but a repeated return to it."[29] Thus Trigg continues to describe the circular nature of baptismal life in Luther's thought as this is expressed in the catechisms:

---

27   Bayer, *Luther's Theology*, 268. Also note Luther: "In baptism, therefore, every Christian has enough to study and practice all his or her life. Christians always have enough to do to believe firmly what baptism promises and brings—victory over death and the devil, forgiveness of sin, God's grace, the entire Christ, and the Holy Spirit with his gifts. In short, the blessings of baptism are so boundless that if our timid nature considers them, it may well doubt whether they could all be true" (LC IV 41–42; K-W 461).

28   Luther: "I say this to correct the opinion, which has long prevailed among us, that baptism is something past that we can no longer use after falling back into sin. This idea comes from looking only at the act that took place a single time. Indeed, St. Jerome is responsible for this view, for he wrote, 'Penance is the second plank on which we must swim ashore after the ship founders,' [the ship] in which we embarked when we entered the Christian community. This takes away the value of baptism, making it of no further use to us. Therefore it is incorrect to say this. The ship does not break up because, as we said, it is God's ordinance and not something that is ours. But it does happen that we slip and fall out of the ship. However, those who do fall out should immediately see to it that they swim to the ship and hold fast to it, until they can climb aboard again and sail on in it as before" (LC IV 80–82; K-W 466).

29   Jonathan Trigg, *Baptism in the Theology of Martin Luther* (Leiden: Brill, 2001), 96. Such a return to Baptism is necessary because of the continuing reality of sin in the believer's life: "This continuation

Luther imposes a circular shape upon the Christian life. The Christian must never presume to claim any achievement or progress which places him beyond the call for a continual repentance of the past in *toto*, and a repeated return to the promise of righteousness in Christ—to the promise of baptism itself. The "circular" shape of the Christian life and the present tense of baptism are inextricably linked; baptism, even though it is administered only once, does not lose force after post-baptismal sin, as has for so long been held.[30]

The only way to live in Baptism is by repentance and faith. This is the continual return to Baptism.

Prayer lives by always returning to Baptism, saying "Amen" to God's work of breaking and hindering "every evil plan and purpose of the devil, the world, and our sinful nature, which do not want us to hallow God's name or let His kingdom come," to use the words of Luther's explanation of the Third Petition of the Lord's Prayer. This is repentance. On the basis of God's reliable promise in Baptism, we can count on Him to strengthen and keep us "firm in His Word and faith until we die." This is God's good and gracious will. We return to our Baptism when we pray, "Thy will be done."

How seriously Luther takes Baptism we can see from his *Baptismal Booklet*,[31] which was originally published in 1523. In 1526 it was included with his revised baptismal rite, and later it was appended to editions of the Small Catechism. In this booklet Luther urges that continual prayers be made for those who are baptized. Sponsors especially are urged to pray for those they bring to the font. Recalling the prayers of the baptismal liturgy, Luther writes:

> For here in the words of these prayers you hear how plaintively and earnestly the Christian church brings the infant to God, confesses

---

of sin and evil in the lives of God's chosen people remains a mystery, beyond human solution in this life. Adam and Eve passed on this refusal to trust God to all their descendants in a way that is more profound than human reason or explanations can fathom or express" (Robert Kolb, "The Lutheran Doctrine of Original Sin," in *Adam, the Fall, and Original Sin: Theological, Biblical, and Scientific Perspectives*, ed. Hans Madueme and Michael Reeves [Grand Rapids: Baker Academic, 2014], 114).

30 Trigg, *Baptism in the Theology of Martin Luther*, 96.

31 For a thorough presentation on the background of this booklet and its significance, see Albrecht Peters, *Confession and Christian Life*, trans. Thomas H. Trapp, Commentary on Luther's Catechisms 5 (St. Louis: Concordia, 2013), 191–234. In this booklet Luther explains his rationale for streamlining the rite, removing unnecessary ceremonies that tended to cloud God's activity in the sacrament. For more on this point, see also Bryan Spinks, *Reformation and Modern Rituals and Theologies of Baptism: From Luther to Contemporary Practices* (Burlington, VT: Ashgate, 2006), 9–14.

before him with such unchanging, undoubting words that the infant is possessed by the devil and a child of sin and wrath, and so diligently asks for help and grace through baptism, that the infant may become a child of God.[32]

Baptism is no joke, for in this Sacrament a child of Adam becomes a child of God and thus acquires an enemy in the evil one.

Thus it is extremely necessary to stand by the poor child with all your heart and with a strong faith and to plead with great devotion that God, in accordance with these prayers, would not only free the child from the devil's power but also strengthen the child, so that the child might resist him valiantly in life and in death. I fear that people turn out so badly after baptism because we have dealt with them in such a cold and casual way and have prayed for them at their baptism without any zeal at all.[33]

In these prayers, we petition God on behalf of the baptized to do what He has promised in Baptism: to guard and keep those who now bear His name from the devices of Satan who continually seeks to draw Christians out of their Baptism and back into his own dark domain of death and damnation.

---

32   *Baptismal Booklet* 2; K-W 372.

33   *Baptismal Booklet* 3–4; K-W 372.

CHAPTER 6

Confession, Absolution, the Office of the Keys

Absolution Opens Lips for Prayer

INTRODUCTION

"For this is the essence of a genuinely Christian life, to acknowledge that we are sinners and to pray for grace."—Martin Luther[1]

The insertion of a short order of confession between the chief parts on Holy Baptism and the Sacrament of the Altar was intended by Luther to catechize people in the evangelical use of confession and absolution.

Individual confession and absolution is properly placed between Baptism and the Lord's Supper. It marks the point where the *significatio* of Baptism is made specific, the daily drowning of the old man when the guilt is disclosed in the presence of a Christian brother, as well as the daily breaking forth of the new man, empowered by the divine absolution; it is what prepares us for the Lord's Supper.[2]

---

1   LC "Brief Exhortation to Confession" 9; K-W 477.

2   Albrecht Peters, *Confession and Christian Life*, 29.

Anchored in the final section of Baptism—"What does such baptizing with water indicate?"—Luther's treatment demonstrates that to confess one's sins is to return to Baptism in the confidence of God's promise to forgive.

> The eschatological baptismal path for a Christian, to which confession and absolution returns us again and again, is and remains encompassed within and protected by God's faithfulness to His gracious promise.[3]

The original formulation of the catechism did not contain material on confession or the Office of the Keys. The brief order for confession was added in June 1529. The questions were added to the brief order in 1531. The Office of the Keys is derived from the work of Andreas Osiander (ca. 1496–1552) and was included in editions of the catechism already in Luther's lifetime.[4]

Luther certainly did not want to jettison the practice of individual confession, but filter it through the evangelical sieve of justification by faith alone, so that purified from its Roman abuses it might be restored as a means of consolation for those terrified by their sin. In the Smalcald Articles, Luther reflects this evangelical orientation present in the catechism:

> Because absolution or the power of the keys is also a comfort and help against sin and a bad conscience and was instituted by Christ in the gospel, confession, or absolution, should by no means be allowed to fall into disuse in the church—especially for the sake of weak consciences and for the wild young people, so that they may be examined and instructed in Christian teaching.[5]

Ronald Rittgers observes:

> Luther and his early followers loathed the late-medieval version of private confession. However, it is important that we understand the

---

3   Peters, *Confession and Christian Life*, 74.

4   Here see Robert Hinckley, "Andreas Osiander and the Fifth Chief Part," *Logia* 10, no. 4 (Reformation 2001): 37–42. Hinckley notes: "Osiander's explanation of the office of the keys had great impact upon the catechisms of his time, and is responsible for establishing the long-standing tradition among Lutheran catechisms concerning this teaching. The addition of John 20 and Osiander's 'office of the keys' to the confession and absolution created a fifth chief part in the Small Catechism, so that the Sacrament of the Altar became the sixth" ("Osiander and the Fifth Chief Part," 38). For more on this history, see Ronald K. Rittgers, *The Reformation of the Keys: Confession, Conscience, and Authority in Sixteenth-Century Germany* (Cambridge, MA: Harvard University Press, 2004).

5   SA III VIII 1; K-W 321.

source of their animosity. Luther and his fellow reformers attacked confession not because they opposed the practice as such, but because they believed it had been corrupted. They saw in private confession—in the individual application of the Word to the believer—the most effective way of preaching the Gospel to troubled souls.[6]

This is demonstrated in Luther's "Brief Exhortation to Confession" included in the Large Catechism.

In this exhortation, reworked from a 1529 Palm Sunday sermon, Luther argues that confession should not be set aside in the name of Christian freedom. This would be an abuse of liberty that separates the Christian from the very word that brings freedom from sin, namely, the absolution.[7] Instead, burdened consciences should not be tortured with the unreasonable demand to enumerate all their offenses; rather, they should name only those sins which they know and feel. Individual confession rightly takes its place alongside other forms of confession such as we make in the Lord's Prayer, which Luther sees as a "public, daily, and necessary confession."[8] Luther is adamant in his refusal to make individual confession a legal requirement because this would make of the evangelical gift an occasion for coercion and hypocrisy. Instead, Luther urges that "we teach what a wonderful, precious, and comforting thing confession is, and we urge that such a precious blessing should not be despised, especially when we consider our great need."[9] Confession should not be a tool of torture but a means of relief for broken sinners.

Confession should not be a tool of torture but a means of relief for broken sinners.

The practice of confession and absolution is anchored in the preceding portions of the Small Catechism:

> Third Article: "In this Christian church He daily and richly forgives all my sins and the sins of all believers."

---

6   Ronald K. Rittgers, "Private Confession in the German Reformation," in *Repentance in Christian Theology*, ed. Mark J. Boda and Gordon T. Smith, pp. 194–95. Copyright 2006 by Order of Saint Benedict. Published by Liturgical Press, Collegeville, Minnesota. Reprinted with permission.

7   Thus Peters writes: "Whoever was seeking to use their evangelical freedom as freedom *from* our existence under God's Gospel and commandment should be cast once again under the chastening rod of the Law, as well as under God's satanic jailer. By contrast, whoever allows himself to be encouraged and summoned is to experience in this specific activity the full extent of the Gospel, without being treated harshly" (*Confession and Christian Life*, 7).

8   LC "Brief Exhortation to Confession" 13; K-W 477.

9   LC "Brief Exhortation to Confession" 28; K-W 479.

Fifth Petition: "We are neither worthy of the things for which we pray, nor have we deserved them, but we ask that He would give them all to us by grace, for we daily sin much and surely deserve nothing but punishment."

Fourth Part of Holy Baptism: "[Baptism] indicates that the Old Adam in us should by daily contrition and repentance be drowned and die with all sins and evil desires, and that a new man should daily emerge and arise to live before God in righteousness and purity forever."

Confession is made on the basis of the Ten Commandments.

What is Confession?
Confession has two parts.

First, that we confess our sins, and

second, that we receive absolution, that is, forgiveness, from the pastor as from God Himself, not doubting, but firmly believing that by it our sins are forgiven before God in heaven.

What sins should we confess?
Before God we should plead guilty of all sins, even those we are not aware of, as we do in the Lord's Prayer; but before the pastor we should confess only those sins which we know and feel in our hearts.

Which are these?
Consider your place in life according to the Ten Commandments: Are you a father, mother, son, daughter, husband, wife, or worker? Have you been disobedient, unfaithful, or lazy? Have you been hot-tempered, rude, or quarrelsome? Have you hurt someone by your words or deeds? Have you stolen, been negligent, wasted anything, or done any harm?

A SHORT FORM OF CONFESSION

The penitent says:
Dear confessor, I ask you please to hear my confession and to pronounce forgiveness in order to fulfill God's will.

I, a poor sinner, plead guilty before God of all sins. In particular I confess before you that as a servant, maid, etc., I, sad to say, serve my master unfaithfully, for in this and that I have not done what I was told to do. I have made him angry and caused him to curse. I have been negligent and allowed damage to be done. I have also been offensive in words and deeds. I have quarreled with my peers. I have grumbled about the lady of the house and cursed her. I am sorry for all of this and I ask for grace. I want to do better.

A master or lady of the house may say:
In particular I confess before you that I have not faithfully guided my children, servants, and wife to the glory of God. I have cursed. I have set a bad example by indecent words and deeds. I have hurt my neighbor and spoken evil of him. I have overcharged, sold inferior merchandise, and given less than was paid for.

[Let the penitent confess whatever else he has done against God's commandments and his own position.]

If, however, someone does not find himself burdened with these or greater sins, he should not trouble himself or search for or invent other sins, and thereby make confession a torture. Instead, he should mention one or two that he knows: In particular I confess that have cursed; I have used improper words; I have neglected this or that, etc. Let that be enough.

But if you know of none at all (which hardly seems possible), then mention none in particular, but receive the forgiveness upon the general confession which you make to God before the confessor.

Then the confessor shall say:
God be merciful to you and strengthen your faith. Amen.

Furthermore:
Do you believe that my forgiveness is God's forgiveness?

Yes, dear confessor.

Then let him say:
Let it be done for you as you believe. And I, by the command of our Lord Jesus Christ, forgive you your sins in the name of the Father and of the Son and of the Holy Spirit. Amen. Go in peace.

A confessor will know additional passages with which to comfort and to strengthen the faith of those who have great burdens of conscience or are sorrowful and distressed.

This is intended only as a general form of confession.

What is the Office of the Keys?
The Office of the Keys is that special authority which Christ has given to His church on earth to forgive the sins of repentant sinners, but to withhold forgiveness from the unrepentant as long as they do not repent.

Where is this written?
This is what St. John the Evangelist writes in chapter twenty: The Lord Jesus breathed on His disciples and said, "Receive the Holy Spirit. If you forgive anyone his sins, they are forgiven; if you do not forgive them, they are not forgiven." (John 20:22–23)

What do you believe according to these words?
I believe that when the called ministers of Christ deal with us by His divine command, in particular when they

exclude openly unrepentant sinners from the Christian congregation and absolve those who repent of their sins and want to do better, this is just as valid and certain, even in heaven, as if Christ our dear Lord dealt with us Himself.

Holy and merciful Father, You teach us that if we do not confess our sins, the truth is not in us. Grant us honest hearts to plead guilty of all sins, even those of which we are unaware—as we do in the Lord's Prayer—but also give us courage to confess before the pastor those sins which we know and feel in our hearts. Having confessed our sins, give us ears to hear and hearts to receive Your absolution, that is, forgiveness, from the pastor as from You Yourself, not doubting but firmly believing that by it, our sins are forgiven before You in heaven; through Jesus Christ, Your Son, our Lord, who lives and reigns with You and the Holy Spirit, one God, now and forever. Amen.

Confession embraces the recognition and naming of sins and the word of God's forgiveness of sins for the sake of Christ, the absolution. In contrast to the Roman Catholic practice, Luther shifts the emphasis from the act of confession to the speaking of the word of divine forgiveness. As Werner Klän observes: "Luther's concept of confession and repentance is marked by a dual structure consisting of human and divine actions, wherein the divine action carries the whole weight."[10]

Confession and absolution are an exercise in the ministry of the Law and the Gospel. Through the Law one is brought to know his sins and is crushed with the recognition of their condemning consequences before God. The heart broken by the Law can only acknowledge that God's verdict is true. This knowledge of sin, Luther says in his 1532 lectures on Psalm 51, "means to feel and to experience the intolerable burden of the wrath of God."[11] Such a heart has nowhere to turn except to the promise of God: "A broken and contrite heart, O God, You will

---

10   Werner Klän, "The 'Third Sacrament': Confession and Repentance in the Confessions of the Lutheran Church," trans. Mathias Hohls, *Logia* 20, no. 3 (Holy Trinity 2011): 5. Also see Luther in the Large Catechism: "Note, then, as I have often said, that confession consists of two parts. The first is our work and act, when I lament my sin and desire comfort and restoration for my soul. The second is the work that God does, when he absolves me of my sins through the Word placed on the lips of another person. This is the surpassingly grand and noble thing that makes confession so wonderful and comforting" (LC Brief Exhortation to Confession 15; K-W 478).

11   *Commentary on Psalm 51* (1532/1538), AE 12:310.

not despise" (Psalm 51:17). To this broken heart, incapable of mending itself, the absolution is spoken as the purest and most concentrated form of the Gospel: "I forgive you your sins."

Confession makes of us beggars before God. The divine wisdom of the Gospel is that God is merciful to sinners for the sake of Christ Jesus. To confess one's sins is to make supplication to God for mercy. To pray for mercy as David does in Psalm 51 is not to trust in oneself or one's own works. Luther says, "God does not want the prayer of a sinner who does not feel his sins, because he neither understands nor wants what he is praying for."[12] Such praying, Luther contends, is to be compared to a beggar who cries out for alms and when offered money begins to brag of his riches.

> Thus mercy is our whole life even until death; yet Christians yield obedience to the Law, but imperfect obedience because of the sin dwelling in us. For this reason let us learn to extend the word "Have mercy" not only to our actual sins but to all the blessings of God as well: that we are righteous by the merit of another; that we have God as our Father; that God the Father loves sinners who feel their sins—in short, that all our life is by mercy because all our life is sin and cannot be set against the judgment and wrath of God.[13]

David is like a beggar: he asks for forgiveness for no other reason than that he is a sinner.

To confess your sin is to cease the futile attempt to self-justify. Rather, it is to join with David in saying to God: "Against You, You only, have I sinned and done what is evil in Your sight, so that You may be justified in Your words and blameless in Your judgment" (Psalm 51:4). In confession, the sinner acknowledges that God is right. It is to agree with God's verdict: guilty.

> When sins are thus revealed by the Word, two different kinds of men manifest themselves. One kind justifies God and by a humble confession agrees to His denunciation of sin; the other kind condemns God and calls Him a liar when He denounces sin.[14]

Confession of sin is the opposite of self-justification.

---

12 *Commentary on Psalm 51* (1532/1538), AE 12:315.

13 *Commentary on Psalm 51* (1532/1538), AE 12:320–21.

14 *Commentary on Psalm 51* (1532/1538), AE 12:341.

Confession of sins before God, from whom no secrets are hidden, is inclusive as "we should plead guilty of all sins, even . . . as we do in the Lord's Prayer." This acknowledgment of sin recognizes its totality and admits no righteousness before God. But before the pastor, Luther asserts, "we should confess only those sins which we know and feel in our hearts." These sins are brought to light in the self-examination that takes stock of one's life as it is evaluated from the perspective of the intersection of God's Law (Ten Commandments) and one's "place in life," that is, one's calling.[15] Confession is not a meritorious act that becomes the cause of forgiveness. Rather, "the purpose of confession is to disclose sin in order that it may be forgiven, not to glorify our contrition."[16] Luther saw confession in light of the words of Psalm 32:3: "For when I kept silent, my bones wasted away through my groaning all day long." The disclosure of sin brings it to light, thus depriving it of its cancerous capacity to gnaw away at the life of the believer and hold him within its lethal grasp. "Bringing it out into the open deprives sin of its power."[17] Left unconfessed, sin festers, promoting denial and suppression. This dynamic is broken as sin is laid out before the confessor where it can be addressed directly by God's absolution. Confession without absolution would be devoid of Christ and end in either pride or despair—both of which are damning.

> *Confession makes of us beggars before God.*

Therefore, Luther moves quickly from the act of confession to the absolution, the word of forgiveness on the lips of the pastor that is God's own word. Luther's aim is that the penitent would know and trust the evangelical word of absolution. At this stage in the catechism, Luther has little to say about confession—he simply says "that we are to confess our sins"—but instead he weighs in on the absolution, what it is and how we are to receive it. If the Law brings about despair, then the Gospel spoken in the absolution delivers comfort, which, as Berndt Hamm points out, is, for Luther, a "comforted despair."[18]

---

15   Here note Peters: "Our confession before God is to be comprehensive and complete, but it is to concentrate on specific offenses when it is uttered before human beings. Luther brings this into one's awareness by linking the Old Testament Decalogue with the New Testament Household Responsibilities, which demarcate our 'estate'—our God-ordained standing within the coordinated system that exists among human beings" (*Confession and Christian Life*, 9).

16   Herbert Girgensohn, *Teaching Luther's Catechism*, 2:77. Helpful here is "Preparation for Confession and Absolution According to the Ten Commandments," in *A Treasury of Daily Prayer*, gen. ed. Scot A. Kinnaman (St. Louis: Concordia, 2008), 1460–62, which is also included as an appendix of this book.

17   Girgensohn, *Teaching Luther's Catechism*, 2:69.

18   Berndt Hamm, *The Early Luther: Stages in Reformation Reorientation*, trans. Martin J. Lohrmann (Grand Rapids: Eerdmans, 2014), 131.

Where the accent is on the act of confession—was it comprehensive enough to name all sins, was it sincerely made, was it motivated out of a pure love of God—the conscience is left unprotected from the monster of uncertainty.[19] One can then never have the assurance that God has forgiven his sins.[20] For Luther, the only certainty is in the word and work of God that is going on in the words spoken by the pastor whereby "we receive absolution, that is, forgiveness, from the pastor as from God Himself." Here God would graciously interfere with our doubting so that we firmly believe that by the absolution, we know "our sins are forgiven before God in heaven." It is in this sense that "private confession exists for the sake of the certainty of salvation."[21]

There is nothing conditional about the absolution; it is the trustworthy verdict of the triune God spoken by the pastor to be received by faith. "There is no such thing as a hypothetical absolution."[22] As Oswald Bayer has demonstrated, the absolution is no mere sign pointing to a forgiveness located elsewhere, but rather it is a word that actually carries and bestows the forgiveness of sins:

> That the verbal sign itself is the matter itself, that it presents not an absent but rather a present matter, that was Luther's great hermeneutical discovery, his reformatory discovery in the strict sense of the word. He made this discovery first of all in his investigation of the sacrament of penance (1518). That the sign itself is already the matter and event itself means in view of absolution that the sentence "I absolve you of your sins" is not merely a declaratory judgment of what already is, thus presupposing an inner, proper absolution. The word of absolution is rather a verbal act, which

---

19   Note Luther's comments: "For anyone who has such doubts about the will of God toward him and who does not believe for a certainty that he is in a state of grace cannot believe that he has forgiveness of sins, that God cares about him, or that he can be saved" (*Lectures on Galatians* [1531/1535], AE 26:377).

20   Such was the case, Peters argues, in the Roman Church: "The pressure that had been placed heretofore on the works of the penitent made divine forgiveness dependent upon our having arrived at a sufficient level of sorrow, pushing the anguished soul thereby either into doubt or deluding it into false confidence" (*Confession and Christian Life*, 11).

21   Girgensohn, *Teaching Luther's Catechism*, 2:67. Luther's pastoral aim is that the broken sinner have the certainty of the Gospel. Luther writes: "This is the reason why our theology is certain: it snatches us away from ourselves and places us outside ourselves, so that we do not depend on our own strength, conscience, experience, person, or works but depend on that which is outside ourselves, that is, on the promise and truth of God, which cannot deceive" (*Lectures on Galatians* [1531/1535], AE 26:387).

22   Girgensohn, *Teaching Luther's Catechism*, 2:80.

creates a relationship— between God in whose name it is spoken, and the person to whom it is spoken.[23]

After the questions on confession, Luther inserts a brief order so that Christians might actually make an evangelical use of confession.

> Luther's discussion of confession, along with the shape of his liturgical rite, shows how he redefines its essence and practice so that it ceases to be a burden and instead becomes an instrument by which the Gospel is conveyed personally to an individual.[24]

Luther's rite is simple and straightforward. It opens not with an invitation from the pastor but with the plea of the penitent, imploring the confessor to hear his or her confession and "pronounce forgiveness in order to fulfill God's will." Luther then provides what might be best described as a template or model for the penitent to use in confessing his or her sins. After the admission of guilt "before God of all sins," there is the particular confession of sins according to a specific station in life. Luther pastorally notes that if a person does not find himself or herself burdened with particular sins, none should be invented, nor should the penitent scrutinize the conscience in order to search them out. Neither should the pastor attempt to work as a detective to ferret out offenses. A general confession would be preferable to an invented one.

After the confession is spoken, the pastor blesses the penitent: "God be merciful to you and strengthen your faith." This is followed by the confessional question posed toward the absolution: "Do you believe that my forgiveness is God's forgiveness?" and the anticipated response: "Yes, dear confessor." Then the pastor speaks the absolution. Here the pastor "is not the judge of souls, but the comforter of the conscience that God Himself has stricken."[25] The pastor does not

---

23   Oswald Bayer, "Martin Luther," in *The Reformation Theologians*, ed. Carter Lindberg (Malden, MA: Blackwell, 2002), 54. Also Wilhelm Löhe: "God's Word does not teeter-totter; He cannot be untrue to Himself; what He uttered here on earth is true also for the Last Day; His absolution, which is a whispered breath here, will be a mighty absolution there, against which the gates of hell shall not prevail" (cited in Peters, *Confession and Christian Life*, 43).

24   Charles Arand, *That I May Be His Own*, 169.

25   Peters, *Confession and Christian Life*, 79. Note Luther's language in a 1531 sermon included in Veit Dietrich's *House Postil* in 1544: "For we should beware of mixing the two [governments] and tossing them together, as the pope and his bishops have done, who have used the spiritual government in such a way that they have become worldly lords, and emperors and kings have had to bow before them. This was not Christ's mandate to His disciples, and He did not send them forth for secular government. Rather, He committed to them the preaching office, and with it the government over sin, so that the proper definition of the office of preaching is this: that one should preach the Gospel of Christ and forgive the sins of the

hold the office of judge or executioner, but is instead called to be Christ's voice of reconciliation to bestow the Lord's own verdict of mercy in the forgiveness of sins to those who repent. It is not the job of the pastor to weigh sins or to distinguish what is sinful from what is not. His ears are there to receive the confession; his mouth is there to pronounce Christ's forgiveness. "Not determining sins, but comforting the sinner is the real art and function of the confessor."[26]

The absolution then becomes the basis for pastoral counsel and admonition as Luther notes that the confessor will know additional texts from Holy Scripture to use in consoling those with burdened consciences who are distressed and sorrowful. Such counsel does not supplement the absolution as though the forgiving word of Christ needed an additive of amendment of life to make it complete. Instead, the absolution is the only sure foundation for genuine care of consciences. Werner Klän rightly says:

> Therefore, forgiveness is the epitome of the gospel. It is a complete gift, the conferring of a wholeness that is lacking in our existence. It is an equalization of a deficit, a deficit that makes our lives incomplete in the eyes of God when compared to the measure of his own completeness, with which we ought to comply. In the end, it is all about escape from eternal death, which threatens us as a consequence of God's justified wrath.[27]

The absolution received by faith alone, that is, in the reliance that Jesus' verdict of forgiveness is trustworthy and sufficient, is now the context in which ongoing pastoral care can flourish.

The basis for the practice of individual confession and absolution is found in the Office of the Keys. The language of the Office of the Keys is taken from Matthew 16:13–19 (where Jesus bestows "the keys of the kingdom") and from Matthew 18:18 (where Jesus speaks of binding and loosing sins on earth that are at the same time bound and loosed in heaven). The catechism echoes these pericopes in explaining the power of the Keys, but cites John 20:22–23 as the dominical basis for the forgiving and retaining of sins. This is a power that Christ gives to the whole Church, but it is publicly exercised by His called servants as

---

crushed, fearful consciences, but retain those of the impenitent and secure, and bind them" (sermon for April 16, 1531, AE 69:383).

26   Edmund Schlink, *Theology of the Lutheran Confessions*, trans. Paul F. Koehneke and Herbert J. A. Bouman (St. Louis: Concordia, 2003), 139.

27   Klän, " 'Third Sacrament,' " 9.

they "deal with us by His divine command." This divine forgiveness is not locked away in the secrecy of the heavenly chambers, and it is not to be sought there. Rather, God locates this celestial gift here on earth. In his 1536 sermon on John 20:19–31, Luther says:

> [But Christ says:] "Do not gape toward heaven when you want remission of sins. Rather, you have it here below. If [you have] a pastor, or a neighbor in a case of need, there is no need to seek the Absolution from above, because this Absolution spoken on earth is Mine. Why? Because I have so instituted it, and My resurrection will effect it. Therefore, no one will accuse you, neither death nor the devil nor I Myself, when you have received this Absolution, since it is God's own," etc. It is true that God alone forgives sins, [but] how will I get to heaven? There is no need. Go to the pastor; in case of need, tell your neighbor to recite the Absolution in the name of Jesus Christ. Then you have the Word; when they do it, Christ has done it.[28]

Because it is Christ's word, the absolution is sure and certain.

It is only in the surety of sins forgiven that we can call God "our Father" with boldness and confidence. Confession of sins speaks the truth about who we are and what we have done. The silence is broken, and the heart is laid bare before the omniscient Lord. Confession, as Luther envisioned it, does not leave the sinner to deal with sins the best he or she can. Nor is the sinner left with the cruel and ultimately blasphemous advice of pop psychology:

Because it is Christ's word, the absolution is sure and certain.

"You must learn to forgive yourself." Self-forgiveness is an exercise that embodies either despair or presumption as it causes the sinner to pretend that he or she is, in fact, God. God alone has the power to forgive sins. This He has done by His own suffering and death for the sins of the world. The forgiveness accomplished at Calvary, announced at Easter, is now contained in the words spoken by the Lord's servant: "Your sins are forgiven you." It is that word which opens the heart and unlocks the lips for prayer, praise, and thanksgiving as Luther demonstrates in the final stanza of his hymnic paraphrase of Psalm 130:

28   Sermon for April 23, 1536, AE 69:416.

Though great our sins, yet greater still
Is God's abundant favor;
His hand of mercy never will
Abandon us, nor waver.
Our shepherd good and true is He,
Who will at last His Israel free
From all their sin and sorrow. (*LSB* 607:5)

CHAPTER 7

The Sacrament of the Altar

The Promise From Which Prayer Flows

The Lord's Supper is Christ's gift and testament; it is not to be confused with our prayers.[1] One of the venerable names for the Sacrament of the Altar, "Eucharist," is apt to mislead, for this title is derived from the Greek word that means "to give thanks." Surely the gift of Jesus' body and blood is the cause for profound thanksgiving, but our giving of thanks is in no way to be confused with the gift itself.[2] In our prayers, we give thanks for the benefits of the Lord's Supper, but our praying does not make the Holy Supper what it is. Luther removed the Canon of the Mass from the liturgy not only because it was rife with unbiblical notions of sacrifice but also because it fundamentally confused the Church's praying with God's speaking and giving. Thanksgiving is distinguished from God's giving. Luther removes the Eucharistic Prayer containing the Words of Institution, letting the words of Jesus stand with naked clarity as the words that consecrate the bread and wine and thus bestow Christ's body and blood, proclaiming the forgiveness of

---

1   See *Babylonian Captivity* (1520): "We must therefore sharply distinguish the testament and sacrament itself from the prayers which we offer at the same time" (AE 36:50).

2   Wilfried Härle is right to assert: "I am deliberately not using the widespread term 'eucharist' (='thanksgiving'), which arose in the second century (Didache 9,1 and 5; Ignatius' Letter to Ephesians 13,1) and depended upon the liturgical prominence of the consecration of the bread in the Lord's Supper (1 Cor. 11:24). The term 'eucharist' has admittedly found wide acceptance in ecumenical circles, but as a term, it has only an unspecific, and thus misleading, relationship to the origin and meaning of the Lord's Supper. Its use can give rise to the impression that the essential feature of the Lord's Supper is the congregation's giving of thanks" (*Outline of Christian Doctrine*, trans. Ruth Yule and Nicholas Sagovsky [Grand Rapids: Eerdmans, 2015], 454).

sins. Thanksgiving, though, is not removed from the liturgy; rather, it is relocated in the post-Communion collect:

> We give thanks to You, almighty God, that You have refreshed us through this salutary gift, and we implore You that of Your mercy You would strengthen us through the same in faith toward You and in fervent love toward one another; through Jesus Christ, Your Son, our Lord, who lives and reigns with You and the Holy Spirit, one God, now and forever.[3]

This collect composed by Luther is the real Eucharistic Prayer in the Lutheran liturgy because it gives thanks to God for the salutary gift of Christ's body and blood and implores Him that this gift would strengthen us in faith toward Him and love toward one another. Eucharist, or the giving of thanks, is not to be confused with the Lord's Supper; rather, it flows from it. The Small Catechism demonstrates how this is so.

Luther's pastoral goal was that Christians know what the Sacrament is, its benefits, and how it is to be used in faith. The Sacrament is established by the Word of Christ and is to be used according to His Word:

> All this is established from the words Christ used to institute it. So everyone who wishes to be a Christian and to go to the sacrament should know them. For we do not intend to admit to the sacrament and administer it to those who do not know what they seek or why they come.[4]

Through this teaching, believers are guarded against understandings of the Sacrament that contradict the clear meaning of the Lord's words, and they are tutored in how to make use of Christ's gift in faith and so receive the blessings He has placed there.

The catechisms were written after more than a decade of struggle involving the Lord's Supper. This was a battle that the reformer had to fight on two fronts. On one side was the Roman Catholic Church; on the other were those associated with Ulrich Zwingli and the so-called Sacramentarians, who thought that Luther's teaching did not go far enough in divesting the Lord's Supper of Roman errors and restoring it to a genuine remembrance of Christ. The catechisms, each in its own way, sought to address the errors of both groups.

---

3 *LSB*, p. 201.
4 LC V 1–2; K-W 467.

For the Roman Church, the key category for the Sacrament was that of sacrifice. While Luther also recognized other crucial errors (including the teaching of transubstantiation and the withholding of the chalice from the laity), the notion of sacrifice was the chief error because it reversed the direction of the Sacrament so that instead of Christ's body and blood being a testament received for the forgiveness of sins, it became a ritual work done to merit grace. Early in the controversy with Rome and consistently thereafter, Luther insisted that the Sacrament and sacrifice must be kept distinct.[5] Luther held that the Roman doctrine of transubstantiation was an unbiblical and clumsy philosophical attempt to explain how Christ's body and blood are present in the Sacrament, but he did agree with Rome that Christ's body and blood are present. They are present, however, not as an offering to God but as God's gracious testament to sinners to be received in faith.

On the other side of the battlefield were the Sacramentarians, who denied the bodily presence of the crucified and risen Christ under the bread and the wine. For them the Lord's Supper was not the testament of the forgiveness of sins bestowed in the Lord's body and blood under bread and wine, but an ordinance to remember Christ and partake of Him by obedient faith in thanksgiving.

Charles Arand observes that the Small Catechism addresses both of these errant positions: the questions "What is the Sacrament of the Altar?" and "How can bodily eating and drinking do such great things?" are aimed primarily at the Sacramentarians, and the questions "What is the benefit of this eating and drinking?" and "Who receives this sacrament worthily?" address the Roman Church.[6] With brevity and without polemic, Luther crafts a compact confession of the Lord's Supper that is remarkable for its clarity and fullness. With an economy of words, Luther answers his opponents, but more than that, he provides a clear definition of the Sacrament, accents its benefits for faith, and addresses its use by believers, all while keeping his explanation firmly anchored to Jesus' words.

What is the Sacrament of the Altar?
It is the true body and blood of our Lord Jesus Christ
under the bread and wine, instituted by Christ
Himself for us Christians to eat and to drink.

---

5   See *Treatise on the New Testament* (1520) (AE 35:99). See also Carl Wisløff, *The Gift of Communion: Luther's Controversy with Rome on Eucharistic Sacrifice*, trans. Joseph Shaw (Minneapolis: Augsburg, 1964).

6   Charles Arand, *That I May Be His Own*, 171.

Where is this written?

The holy Evangelists Matthew, Mark, Luke, and St. Paul write:

Our Lord Jesus Christ, on the night when He was betrayed, took bread, and when He had given thanks, He broke it and gave it to the disciples and said: "Take, eat; this is My body, which is given for you. This do in remembrance of Me."

In the same way also He took the cup after supper, and when He had given thanks, He gave it to them, saying, "Drink of it, all of you; this cup is the new testament in My blood, which is shed for you for the forgiveness of sins. This do, as often as you drink it, in remembrance of Me."

Lord Jesus Christ, on the solemn night of Your betrayal, You established the Sacrament, giving us Your true body and blood under bread and wine for us Christians to eat and drink. We praise You for this wondrous testament and pray that You would lead us to eat and drink Your body and blood, trusting in Your promise alone; for You live and reign with the Father and the Holy Spirit, ever one God. Amen.

Luther defines the Sacrament of the Altar with clarity and simplicity as Christ's true body and blood under bread and wine for us Christians to eat and drink. The words Jesus used in instituting the Sacrament tell us what it is. Not only in the opening section of the sixth chief part but in each of the remaining sections, the *Verba testament*, the Words of the Lord, are Luther's point of departure and return. Albrecht Peters correctly concludes:

> It may be true that Luther points tirelessly to the Words of Institution, but he makes sure that everything is dealt with on a pure, exegetical level and insists on using nothing other than the clear wording of the text that is attested unanimously.[7]

---

7   Albrecht Peters, *Baptism and Lord's Supper*, 150. Also note Peters's remark: "The reformer extracts from the Words of Institution both the substance of and the fruit of the Lord's Supper" (152).

There are no dogmatic theories of sacramental presence trotted out by the reformer, just an appeal to Jesus' trustworthy words.

By virtue of His almighty word, Jesus gives His true body and blood under bread and wine for Christians to eat and drink in this Sacrament. Catechetically, no other explanations are necessary. Christ's words bestow what they promise. Bread and wine are not symbols for an otherwise absent body and blood. Yet the bread and wine do not cease to be bread and wine. Under these creaturely elements, Christ gives His crucified and risen body. The words of Luther's hymn make it clear that the body and blood given under bread and wine are the body and blood born of Mary and crucified for us:

Christ's words bestow what they promise.

> O Lord, we praise Thee, bless Thee, and adore Thee,
> In thanksgiving bow before Thee.
> Thou with Thy body and Thy blood didst nourish
> Our weak souls that they may flourish: O Lord, have mercy!
> May Thy body, Lord, born of Mary,
> That our sins and sorrows did carry,
> And Thy blood for us plead
> In all trial, fear, and need: O Lord, have mercy! (*LSB* 617:1)

He gives His true body and blood, the catechism says, for us Christians to eat and drink. It is not given as a manifestation of the divine presence to be housed for ritual adoration. It is not given that it may be represented to God as a sacrifice. It is there for eating and drinking that Christians might be strengthened in their faith.

What is the benefit of this eating and drinking?

These words, "Given and shed for you for the forgiveness of sins," show us that in the Sacrament forgiveness of sins, life, and salvation are given us through these words. For where there is forgiveness of sins, there is also life and salvation.

Your holy words, Lord Jesus, "given and shed for you for the forgiveness of sins," bestow on all who believe forgiveness of sins in which there is life with You and salvation in the resurrection of our bodies. Cause us to cling to Your words and so know that, on account of Your Passion, our sins are forgiven, our lives are redeemed from death, and our destiny in Your heavenly kingdom is made certain; for You live and reign with the Father and the Holy Spirit, ever one God. Amen.

—————————∞⟨⟩∞—————————

The benefit of eating and drinking in the Sacrament is identified by Jesus' words "Given and shed for you for the forgiveness of sins." With these words we are drawn back to the catechism's exposition of the Second Article of the Creed with its confession that Christ has redeemed us, that is, purchased and won us from "all sins, from death, and from the power of the devil." His redemptive work is summarized in the single phrase "for the forgiveness of sins." What was accomplished on the cross is now delivered in the Lord's Supper.

The forgiveness of sins lies at the heart of the Sacrament. Luther drives this home with the triple repetition of "given for you" and "shed for the forgiveness of sins" in the sixth chief part. Oswald Bayer observes:

> Luther does not concentrate on the threefold repetition of the two phrases "given for you" and "shed for the forgiveness of sins" just by chance. God's turning toward the sinner, the promise that creates faith, empowered by the death and resurrection of Jesus Christ, cannot be summarized any more succinctly and specifically than by using these words. This must be stated clearly as a critique of the depersonalizing speech about the "bread of life" or the diminution of the Lord's Supper to become a generic lovefest. The Lord's Supper is not some diffuse celebration of life but is defined in a precise way in its essence by means of the connection between the Word of Christ that has effective power and the faith.[8]

The Lord's Supper is tied up with the cross.

The body and blood of Christ sacrificed on Good Friday are now given us to eat and to drink for the forgiveness of sins.

---

8   Bayer, *Luther's Theology*, 272. Also see Kenneth F. Korby: "The forgiveness of sin is both the beginning and the goal. We do not start with the forgiveness and then move on to something higher, greater, or better. The East saw the gift of immortal life as the gift of the Eucharist. The West saw the immaculate offering of the church to her Lord—but in the communion only an appendix with the forgiveness of sins (but not of mortal sins so as not to degenerate the sacrament of penance). The mystics saw in the Lord's Supper the mystery-laden liquefaction of the individual in the awe. But Luther concentrates on the center, the forgiveness of sin" ("The Use of John 6 in Lutheran Sacramental Piety," in *Shepherd the Church: Essays in Honor of the Rev. Dr. Roger D. Pittelko*, ed. Frederic Baue et al. [Fort Wayne: Concordia Theological Seminary Press, 2002], 131–32).

Therefore it is absurd for them to say that Christ's body and blood are not given and poured out for us in the Lord's Supper and hence that we cannot have forgiveness of sins in the sacrament. Although the work took place on the cross and forgiveness of sins has been acquired, yet it cannot come to us in any other way than through the Word.[9]

A few years earlier, in 1525, Luther had stated the same thing with even more force in *Against the Heavenly Prophets*:

If now I seek the forgiveness of sins, I do not run to the cross, for I will not find it given there. Nor must I hold to the suffering of Christ, as Dr. Karlstadt trifles, in knowledge or remembrance, for I will not find it there either. But I will find in the sacrament or gospel the word which distributes, presents, offers, and gives to me that forgiveness which was won on the cross.[10]

Earlier in his career, Luther had focused on the word *testament* (*diatheke*) as this term entails the character of the gift given in the Lord's Supper.[11] While Luther does not give an explicit treatment of this word in the catechisms, it certainly informs his description of the benefits of the Sacrament. Only one who is to die makes a testament, and with it he names the benefits to be distributed to his heirs. So it is with Jesus' institution of the Sacrament of the Altar. "Testament" embraces both incarnation and atonement, Luther argues, for if God is to make such a testament, He must take on flesh and die.[12] Luther sees the Gospel itself as an explanation of this testament.[13] The Sacrament preaches this Gospel so that consciences terrorized by the knowledge of sin and fearful of God's wrath might come to rest in Christ's work of reconciliation. His body and blood proclaims that He is for you and not against you as He extends the forgiveness of sins to all who trust His promise.

---

9   LC V 31; K-W 469.

10   *Against the Heavenly Prophets* (1525), AE 40:214.

11   Here see Reinhard Schwarz, "The Last Supper: The Testament of Jesus," *Lutheran Quarterly* 9 (Winter 1995): 391–404.

12   In *Babylonian Captivity* (1520), Luther noted: "A testator is a promiser who is about to die.... Now God made a testament; therefore, it was necessary that he should die. But God could not die unless he became man. Thus the incarnation and death of Christ are both comprehended most concisely in this one word, 'testament' " (AE 36:38).

13   Luther, *Treatise on the New Testament* (1520): "What is the whole gospel but an explanation of this testament?" (AE 35:106).

The forgiveness of sins is not one among several benefits of the Sacrament. All that Christ has accomplished in His reconciling death and victorious resurrection is encapsulated in that phrase, including life and salvation. Without the forgiveness of sins there is neither life nor salvation. Where there is forgiveness of sins there is also concomitantly life and salvation.

How can bodily eating and drinking do such great things?
Certainly not just eating and drinking do these things, but the words written here: "Given and shed for you for the forgiveness of sins." These words, along with the bodily eating and drinking, are the main thing in the Sacrament. Whoever believes these words has exactly what they say: "forgiveness of sins."

Lord Jesus Christ, as we eat Your holy body and drink Your holy blood, draw our hearts to trust in Your promise that Your body and blood were given and shed for the forgiveness of our sins. Give us the confidence that whoever believes Your words has exactly what they say: "forgiveness of sins"; for You live and reign with the Father and the Holy Spirit, ever one God. Amen.

Luther ties the physical eating and drinking to the words of Christ: "Given and shed for you for the forgiveness of sins." These words demonstrate the purpose of the Lord's Supper. It is not simply eating and drinking but Christ's words of promise. These are words that faith lays hold of so that "whoever believes these words has exactly what they say: 'forgiveness of sins.' " All who come to eat and drink in the Lord's Supper eat and drink Christ's true body and blood, but only those who come with faith in Christ's words receive the blessing of the forgiveness of sins. For those who come in unbelief, their eating and drinking is not a harmless or neutral participation in an empty rite. They, too, eat and drink Christ's body and blood, but they consume it to their detriment.[14]

---

14   Gordon Jensen correctly summarizes the reformer's teaching on this point: "Luther insisted that Christ's flesh is not only of no help to a person, but rather, it was actually poison and death if eaten without faith and the Word (WA 26:353,27–354,8; LW 37:238). Christ's real presence was not only life-giving—it could also be deadly to body and soul" ("Luther and the Lord's Supper," in *The Oxford Handbook of Martin Luther's Theology*, ed. Robert Kolb, Irene Dingel, L'ubomír Batka [Oxford: Oxford University Press, 2014], 327).

The reformer's intention is not to frighten people or to cause them to withdraw from the Lord's Supper; rather, he would have us heed Christ's command and promise with attention to our own neediness so that we are compelled to receive the Sacrament frequently. In the Large Catechism, Luther says, "We must never regard the sacrament as a harmful thing from which we should flee, but as a pure, wholesome, soothing medicine that aids you and gives life in both soul and body. For where the soul is healed, the body is helped as well."[15]

Who receives this sacrament worthily?

Fasting and bodily preparation are certainly fine outward training. But that person is truly worthy and well prepared who has faith in these words: "Given and shed for you for the forgiveness of sins."

But anyone who does not believe these words or doubts them is unworthy and unprepared, for the words "for you" require all hearts to believe.

Lord Christ, grant that we may never come to Your altar trusting in our own righteousness or reliant on our own worthiness. Fasting and bodily preparation are fine outward training to discipline the flesh, but they can never make us worthy in Your eyes. Free us from false belief and misplaced trust, and in Your mercy bring us to repentance, deliver us from doubt, and comfort our consciences with Your forgiveness; for You live and reign with the Father and the Holy Spirit, ever one God. Amen.

Fasting and other forms of physical preparation are helpful outward disciplines. Luther never denies that such exercises are helpful. But they remain penultimate; in and of themselves their observance does not make a "worthy and well-prepared" communicant. What is ultimate is trust in Christ's words "Given and shed for you for the forgiveness of sins." Only the one who believes these words is worthy and well prepared to eat and drink Christ's body and blood. Outward disciplines are not in and of themselves spiritual disciplines. They have usefulness only insofar as they assist the believer in the real spiritual discipline of repentance and faith,

---

15   LC V 68; K-W 474.

recognizing his or her need for Christ on account of sin, death, and the devil, and trusting in the Lord's promise to forgive sin in this Sacrament. No human work can make one prepared for the feast that Christ has prepared by His own Passion. This is brought out in Luther's reworking of a hymn on the Sacrament originally penned by John Hus (1369–1415):

> **Agony and bitter labor**
> **Were the cost of God's high favor;**
> **Do not come if you suppose**
> **You need not Him who died and rose.** (*LSB* 627:6)

In our praying, we give thanks for the gift of the Lord's body and blood, which delivers to us the fruits of His suffering and death. As we come to eat and drink our Lord's body and blood, we implore God to deepen in us the knowledge of His favor in the forgiveness of our sins that we might receive His pardon and peace in this Sacrament and so be enlivened to live in faith toward Him and love toward the neighbor. An aid to such praying is the "Christian Questions with Their Answers" attributed to Luther but in all likelihood from the pen of someone else, perhaps Luther's friend Pastor Johann Lang of Erfurt. Appended to the Small Catechism in 1551, this devotional aid draws on catechetical wording, assisting the communicant in a prayerful self-examination in anticipation of the Sacrament, demonstrating yet another dimension to praying the catechism.

CHAPTER 8

Give Us Our Daily Bread

Morning, Evening, and Mealtime

MORNING PRAYER

**In the morning when you get up, make
the sign of the holy cross and say:**
In the name of the Father and of the + Son
and of the Holy Spirit. Amen.

**Then, kneeling or standing, repeat the Creed and the Lord's
Prayer. If you choose, you may also say this little prayer:**
I thank You, my heavenly Father, through Jesus Christ,
Your dear Son, that You have kept me this night from all
harm and danger; and I pray that You would keep me this
day also from sin and every evil, that all my doings and life
may please You. For into Your hands I commend myself, my
body and soul, and all things. Let Your holy angel be with
me, that the evil foe may have no power over me. Amen.

**Then go joyfully to your work, singing a hymn, like that of the
Ten Commandments, or whatever your devotion may suggest.**

EVENING PRAYER

In the evening when you go to bed, make the sign of the holy cross and say:

In the name of the Father and of the + Son
and of the Holy Spirit. Amen.

Then, kneeling or standing, repeat the Creed and the Lord's Prayer. If you choose, you may also say this little prayer:

I thank You, my heavenly Father, through Jesus Christ, Your dear
Son, that You have graciously kept me this day; and I pray that
You would forgive me all my sins where I have done wrong, and
graciously keep me this night. For into Your hands I commend
myself, my body and soul, and all things. Let Your holy angel be
with me, that the evil foe may have no power over me. Amen.

Then go to sleep at once and in good cheer.

Heavenly Father, in whom we live and move and have our being, Your
name is to be praised from the rising of the sun to its going down. Guard and
bless our coming and going that our lives may be kept safe from sin and the
devil and that awake or asleep we may live in the confidence that our time is in
Your merciful hands; through Jesus Christ, our Lord. Amen.

The explanation of the First Article concludes with the statement "For all this
it is my duty to thank and praise, serve and obey Him." Luther left this assertion
hanging at the end of the explanation. There he gave no instructions regarding
how believers are to thank and praise their Creator or how He is to be served
and obeyed. Now the reformer picks up the thread. The heavenly Father is to be
praised and thanked precisely at those junctures in daily life where it is most clear
that we are creatures: when we wake from sleep and again when we take our rest,
as well as at mealtimes, when we receive nourishment for our bodies. God neither
sleeps nor slumbers (see Psalm 121:3–4), but human beings cannot exist without
the alternation between rest and activity. God does not need food; He does not

suffer from hunger (see Psalm 50:12–13), but without something to eat, human beings starve to death. God is thanked and praised exactly at those times each day when it is evident that we are not the Creator but creatures whose lives are dependent on the God who is the almighty Father, Maker of heaven and earth.

Thanksgiving is spoken to God, acknowledging Him to be the donor of every good and perfect gift. Praise is the proclamation to others—indeed, to the whole creation—of the works the triune God has done.[1] Both thanksgiving and praise are brought together in the catechism's Daily Prayers.

Morning and evening prayers were intended by Luther to serve as a liturgical pattern for how Christians might pray the catechism. This is indicated by the rubric "How the head of the family should teach his household to pray morning and evening." The pattern itself begins with the invocation of the triune name and the sign of the cross and incorporates the Creed and the Lord's Prayer to create a platform for the morning and evening collects. The personal *ordo* concludes with a rubric directed either toward the day's work ("Then go joyfully to your work, singing a hymn, like that of the Ten Commandments, or whatever your devotion may suggest") or toward the night's rest ("Then go to sleep at once and in good cheer"). The Ten Commandments hymn ("These Are the Holy Ten Commands," *LSB* 581) directs us to our vocation where God's Law governs our life and callings within creation. The admonition to go to sleep quickly and with good cheer expresses the confidence of Psalm 4:8: "In peace I will both lie down and sleep; for You alone, O LORD, make me dwell in safety."

Behind Luther's morning and evening prayers stands the traditional Daily Office, which was the backbone of monastic prayer. Robert Kolb observes:

> Vital for [Luther's] theological formation were the seven hours of prayer and other aspects of monastic devotional life. Daily repetition of its liturgies drilled psalms and other portions of Scripture into his head. The failure of these spiritual exercises to ease his unsettled, distressed conscience did not alter the fact that the psalmists' cries of repentance and pleas for mercy sprang automatically out of the thesaurus of his memory for the rest of his life.[2]

---

1   What Hans Walter Wolff says of praise in the Old Testament may be applied to Luther's thought as well: "Where the praise of God is absent, man has misunderstood the discord between his neediness and his capabilities" (*Anthropology of the Old Testament*, trans. Margret Kohl [Philadelphia: Fortress, 1974], 228). Luther will not let the user of the Small Catechism forget the distance between his neediness and his capacity. God alone can be praised as the Lord who fills the needy with good things (cf. Luke 1:53).

2   Robert Kolb, *Luther: Confessor of the Faith*, 27.

Luther's life as a monk had been shaped by the rhythm of the sevenfold Daily Office. While Luther's critique of monasticism was severe, he did not abandon completely the prayers he learned within the Augustinian order; rather, they were salvaged for evangelical usage in the Christian family, as Dorothea Wendebourg notes:

> In the Small Catechism . . . we find a short order for morning and evening prayer, the "blessing for the morning" (*Morgensegen*) and the "blessing for the evening" (*Abendsegen*). These prayers are designed to mark the spiritual beginning and end of each day for the whole family. They are combined with the Lord's Prayer, the Creed, and a hymn: a small breviary for the Christian household. The idea behind this practice is undeniably monastic, and of monastic origin are especially those parts that form the center of the short liturgy: the blessings for morning and evening. The former had been a traditional monastic morning blessing, now used by Luther, with only slight alterations, as the standard morning prayer for "the world," with a parallel version made up for the evening.[3]

The morning and evening prayers themselves bear the deep imprint of the Psalter. Particularly prominent are Psalm 31:5: "Into Your hand I commit my spirit; You have redeemed me, O LORD, faithful God"; and Psalm 91:11: "For He will command His angels concerning you to guard you in all your ways." Filtered from the nighttime prayers of the ancient office of Compline, Luther uses in both the morning and evening prayers biblical language to accent God's faithfulness and protective guardianship against the devil.

---

3   Dorothea Wendebourg, "Luther on Monasticism," *Lutheran Quarterly* 19 (Summer 2005): 140. Wendebourg goes on, in a footnote, to describe how Luther used this traditional monastic material in an evangelical way: "The original prayer came from a Latin collection of late medieval texts and spiritual instructions by the Dutchman Johannes Mauburnus (d. 1501/1502). Here, too, it was to be combined with other liturgical elements, of which Luther kept only the first, an invocation of the Trinity together with the sign of the cross (in Mauburnus the invocation was Christological, followed by the above-mentioned prayer, a petition to the Blessed Virgin Mary asking her blessing, a psalm of praise and a hymn to the Virgin which referred to her as the source of our salvation and praise). In Luther's version the prayer is in German, therefore shorter and stylistically simpler than the original, but in other respects more specific. E.g., Luther gives thanks for 'protection during the night from all perils and dangers' (where Mauburnus has only a general thanksgiving for protection at night), he asks for protection from 'all sin and evil, that my entire life and work please thee' (where Mauburnus asks that 'my service [*servitus*] may be pleasing to thee.' Luther also added a formula of commitment which entrusts one's whole life to God, and a plea for protection by God's guardian angel" (149–50).

The prayers contain both thanksgiving and supplication. Thanksgiving is rendered in the morning that God has kept His child during the night from all harm and danger. In the evening, thanksgiving is made that God has graciously kept the believer. The morning supplication implores God to keep us from sin and evil, that all our doings might please Him. In the evening, the supplication begs for the forgiveness of wrongdoing and implores the Father to keep us through the night. In both prayers, Psalm 31:5 is echoed in the petition of commendation: "For into Your hands I commend myself, my body and soul, and all things."[4] Likewise, both prayers petition God to grant the guardianship of His holy angel, "that the evil foe may have no power over me."

The language of commendation is inclusive, embracing "body and soul, and all things," recalling the confession of the First Article that "God has made me and all creatures; that He has given me my body and soul . . . and still takes care of them." The commendation is into the hands of the Father who "defends me against all danger and guards and protects me from all evil." This is the kind of commendation that Luther teaches under the Second Commandment in the Large Catechism as he instructs Christians to defy the devil by keeping God's holy name on our lips:

> For this purpose it also helps to form the habit of commending ourselves each day to God—our soul and body, spouse, children, servants, and all that we have—for his protection against every conceivable need. This is why the Benedicite, the Gratias, and other evening and morning blessings were introduced and have continued among us.[5]

Awake or asleep, at work or at rest, we live within God's merciful providence as children whose times are in God's hands. Prayer at the beginning and end of the day gratefully acknowledges this, even as we call upon God to guard and direct our lives according to His promises.

> In Luther's Morning and Evening Blessings, human beings who are buffeted with anguish about the world and who desire a place of safety are taken seriously and invited to submit themselves to the

---

4 Here note Hans-Joachim Kraus on the language of commendation in Psalm 31: "Life is delivered into another person's area of power and ownership" (*Psalms 1–59: A Continental Commentary*, trans. Hilton C. Oswald [Minneapolis: Fortress, 1993], 363). Commending ourselves into God's hands is confessing that He has power and ownership over our lives.

5 LC I 73; K-W 395–96.

good gifts of God as those that would come from a father or mother, in order to go to work then with courage or have a chance to rest after work has been concluded.[6]

ASKING A BLESSING

The children and members of the household shall go to the table reverently, fold their hands, and say:
The eyes of all look to You, [O Lord,] and You give them their food at the proper time. You open Your hand and satisfy the desires of every living thing. (Ps. 145:15–16)

Then shall be said the Lord's Prayer and the following:
Lord God, heavenly Father, bless us and these Your gifts which we receive from Your bountiful goodness, through Jesus Christ, our Lord. Amen.

RETURNING THANKS

Also, after eating, they shall, in like manner, reverently and with folded hands say:
Give thanks to the Lord, for He is good. His love endures forever. [He] gives food to every creature. He provides food for the cattle and for the young ravens when they call. His pleasure is not in the strength of the horse, nor His delight in the legs of a man; the Lord delights in those who fear Him, who put their hope in His unfailing love. (Ps. 136:1, 25; 147:9–11)

---

6 Frieder Schulz, "Luther's Household Prayers," in Albrecht Peters, *Confession and Christian Life*, trans. Thomas H. Trapp (St. Louis: Concordia, 2013), 251.

Than shall be said the Lord's Prayer and the following:
We thank You, Lord God, heavenly Father, for all Your
benefits, through Jesus Christ, our Lord, who lives and reigns
with You and the Holy Spirit forever and ever. Amen.

**Gracious Father, in Your bountiful goodness You open Your hand to satisfy
the desires of every living thing. Teach us to reverence You alone as the Giver of
our daily bread and so acknowledge You with thanksgiving and praise; through
Jesus Christ, Your Son, who lives and reigns with You and the Holy Spirit, one
God, now and forever. Amen.**

Commenting on the Fourth Petition of the Lord's Prayer, Ernst Lohmeyer says,
"Bread is prayed for here first because it is holy."[7] Old Jewish prayers acknowledged
God as the one who gives bread and with it sustains life in this world. Without it
we would perish. Daily bread is to be received with reverence because it is holy.
It is instructive that Luther creates something of a miniature liturgy around the
family table. Just as Christians approach the altar with reverence, Luther's rubric
calls on "the children and members of the household" to go "to the table reverently"
and with folded hands. Postures typically associated with the Divine Service are
transported into the everyday space of the family dining room.

Psalm 145:15–16 serves as something of an introit in this *ordo*. The verses
from this psalm are "an expression of God's grace, that in it the creator provides
food as a father provides for his household" and this "means that no one can lay
claim to anything as a right."[8] The use of these verses is reflective of Luther's First
Article confession that God is the benefactor who gives food and drink "only out
of fatherly, divine goodness and mercy, without any merit or worthiness in me."
Before the meal is eaten, there is the praying of the Lord's Prayer and a prayer
of blessing. After the meal, there is thanksgiving to God using Psalm 136:1, 25
and Psalm 147:9–11. Claus Westermann holds that the psalms of praise may be
divided into two categories: declarative and descriptive.[9] Luther uses both categories

---

7   Ernst Lohmeyer, *"Our Father": An Introduction to the Lord's Prayer*, trans. John Bowden (New
York: Harper & Row, 1965), 156.

8   Hans-Joachim Kraus, *Theology of the Psalms*, trans. Keith Crim (Minneapolis: Fortress, 1992), 65.

9   See Claus Westermann, *The Praise of God in the Psalms*, trans. Keith R. Crim (Richmond: John

at this juncture. Psalm 136:1 is declarative: "Give thanks to the Lord, for He is good." Psalm 136:25, "He gives food to every creature," and Psalm 147:9–11, "He provides food for the cattle and for the young ravens when they call. His pleasure is not in the strength of the horse, nor His delight in the legs of a man; the Lord delights in those who fear Him, who put their hope in His unfailing love," are descriptive.[10] The table liturgy concludes with the repetition of the Lord's Prayer and a short trinitarian prayer of thanksgiving.

The catechism table prayers embody the truth of 1 Timothy 4:4–5: "For everything created by God is good, and nothing is to be rejected if it is received with thanksgiving, for it is made holy by the word of God and prayer." The gifts of daily bread can be received with thanksgiving only by those who know the truth that all we have in this body and life are from the hands of our Creator.

Knox Press, 1965), 129–30.

10   These passages are from the NIV.

CHAPTER 9

Table of Duties

Prayer in Our Callings

INTRODUCTION

Christians "serve and obey" God not by withdrawal from the world—as was the case in monasticism—but within the genuine "holy orders" God has instituted: congregation, civil government, and the family. Lying behind the catechism's articulation of the "Table of Duties" (*Die Haustafel*) are the three hierarchies sometimes called estates or orders, which were identified in the medieval tradition as a way of delineating stations or structures of life that human beings occupy within an ordered community. In this ordered community, human beings have the responsibility to discharge particular social duties. Luther used these categories in confessing God's creative work in establishing the places where human life is preserved. The three estates are instituted by God and are upheld by His Word for curbing the effects of sin and for providing arenas for human life to flourish according to His design. As Peters notes: "The structure of the List of Household Responsibilities connects what had been articulated concerning the Fourth and Sixth Commandments with the framework of the three 'holy orders and proper estates.' "[1] The Table of Duties demonstrates the interlocking nature of the First Article with the Decalogue as daily life is sustained and ordered within creation.

In contrast to the monastic notion of the superior form of the spiritual life as an ascetic withdrawal from the earthly and temporal, Luther understood the place of the Christian life to be in the world in these "three fundamental forms

---

1   Peters, *Confession and the Christian Life*, 111.

of life."[2] Lecturing on Psalm 111, Luther said that "these three divine stations continue and remain throughout all kingdoms, as wide as the world and to the end of the world."[3] Luther also wrote of the three estates in *On the Councils and the Church*, where he identified these three hierarchies as "ordained by God," saying that "we need no more; indeed, we have enough and more than enough to do in living aright and resisting the devil in these three."[4] Luther used these three God-ordained estates as a polemic against the self-chosen works of religious orders.

Luther's most succinct treatment of the estates is his summary of the teaching in the *Confession Concerning Christ's Supper* written in 1528, just months before his preparation of the catechism. Here he declared that "the holy orders and true religious institutions established by God are these three: the office of priest, the estate of marriage, the civil government."[5] Faith is not confined to any particular estate but is found in all three orders. Although none of them are paths to righteousness before God, they are the concrete locations where faith is active in love for the well-being of the neighbor.

> Above these three institutions and orders is the common order of Christian love, in which one serves not only the three orders but also serves every needy person in general with all kinds of benevolent deeds, such as feeding the hungry, giving drink to the thirsty, forgiving enemies, praying for all men on earth, suffering all kinds of evil on earth, etc. Behold, all of these are called good and holy works. However, none of these orders is a means of salvation. There remains only one way above them all, viz. faith in Jesus Christ.[6]

These estates were, for Luther, "holy orders," for they were sanctified by God's Word. Every human being, according to Luther, lives in all three estates because everyone is bound by obligations to God and the neighbor. It is the Christian

---

2   Oswald Bayer, *Luther's Theology*, 122. Also see Oswald Bayer, "Nature and Institution: Luther's Doctrine of the Three Estates," in *Freedom in Response: Lutheran Ethics: Sources and Controversies*, trans. Jeffrey Cayzer (Oxford: Oxford University Press, 2007), 90–118. For a later sixteenth-century homiletical treatment of the Table of Duties, see Aegidius Hunnius, *The Christian Table of Duties (1588)*, trans. Paul A. Rydecki (Malone, TX: Repristination Press, 2013). Mark Mattes observes that these callings are the arena for discipleship; see Mattes, "Discipleship in Lutheran Perspective," *Lutheran Quarterly* 26 (Summer 2012): 142–63.

3   *Commentary on Psalm 111* (1530), AE 13:369.

4   *On the Councils and the Church* (1539), AE 41:177.

5   *Confession Concerning Christ's Supper* (1528), AE 37:364.

6   *Confession Concerning Christ's Supper* (1528), AE 37:365.

who by faith recognizes that these estates are created by God and are works of His providential care for the good of His creation. In Luther's view, God is hidden behind the masks of those who fill various stations in the estates, using them as instruments for His ongoing work on behalf of human beings.

To Bishops, Pastors, and Preachers

The overseer must be above reproach, the husband of but one wife, temperate, self-controlled, respectable, hospitable, able to teach, not given to drunkenness, not violent but gentle, not quarrelsome, not a lover of money. He must manage his own family well and see that his children obey him with proper respect. 1 Tim. 3:2–4

He must not be a recent convert, or he may become conceited and fall under the same judgment as the devil. 1 Tim. 3:6

He must hold firmly to the trustworthy message as it has been taught, so that he can encourage others by sound doctrine and refute those who oppose it. Titus 1:9

What the Hearers Owe Their Pastors

The Lord has commanded that those who preach the gospel should receive their living from the gospel. 1 Cor. 9:14

Anyone who receives instruction in the word must share all good things with his instructor. Do not be deceived: God cannot be mocked. A man reaps what he sows. Gal. 6:6–7

The elders who direct the affairs of the church well are worthy of double honor, especially those whose work is preaching and teaching. For the Scripture says, "Do not muzzle the ox while it is treading out the grain," and "The worker deserves his wages." 1 Tim. 5:17–18

We ask you, brothers, to respect those who work hard among you, who are over you in the Lord and who admonish you.

Hold them in the highest regard in love because of their
work. Live in peace with each other. 1 Thess. 5:12–13

Obey your leaders and submit to their authority. They
keep watch over you as men who must give an account.
Obey them so that their work will be a joy, not a burden,
for that would be of no advantage to you. Heb. 13:17

Lord Jesus Christ, Head of Your Body, give us grace to live in Your congregation according to our callings, either as a preacher or a hearer of Your Word. Make all pastors bold to proclaim Your truth, and give all hearers faith to receive Your Word with the humility born of faith and an eagerness to honor and support those who bear the office of preaching. Amen.

According to Luther, already in creation God established the Church as the place of His speaking and of human beings answering. Just as the First Commandment is fundamental and universal, so human beings are created to worship their Creator and cannot escape this demand even when the response is unbelief. In his Genesis lectures, Luther spoke of the establishment of a church "without walls"[7] preceding both the household and state. After the fall, the Church as an order of creation remains, but it is corrupted by unbelief, which is false worship. Rather than clinging to the promise of grace and blessing, human beings exchange the truth of God for the lie and worship of the creature instead of the Creator (see Romans 1:25).

Luther does not use the language of clergy and laity in describing the responsibilities within the congregation. Instead, he speaks of preachers and hearers of the Word of the Lord. The terms *bishop, pastor, preacher* are used interchangeably by Luther as referents to the one New Testament office of the Word and Sacrament. With three texts from the Pastoral Epistles, Luther accents the responsibilities of the office-bearer in both personal life and conduct and public accountability for the sound doctrine.

Pastors owe their hearers the trustworthy preaching of God's Word. Hearers owe their preachers obedience to this Word, the honor and respect that accords

---

7   *Lectures on Genesis* (1535–45/1544–54), AE 1:103.

the office, and financial support, citing apostolic admonition from 1 Corinthians 9:14; Galatians 6:6–7; 1 Timothy 5:17–18; and Hebrews 13:17 to this end.

———————— ∘◦◦ ————————

Of Civil Government

Everyone must submit himself to the governing authorities, for there is no authority except that which God has established. The authorities that exist have been established by God. Consequently, he who rebels against the authority is rebelling against what God has instituted, and those who do so will bring judgment on themselves. For rulers hold no terror for those who do right, but for those who do wrong. Do you want to be free from fear of the one in authority? Than do what is right and he will commend you. For he is God's servant to do you good. But if you do wrong, be afraid, for he does not bear the sword for nothing. He is God's servant, an agent of wrath to bring punishment on the wrongdoer. Rom. 13:1–4

Of Citizens

Give to Caesar what is Caesar's, and to
God what is God's. Matt. 22:21

It is necessary to submit to the authorities, not only because of possible punishment but also because of conscience. This is also why you pay taxes, for the authorities are God's servants, who give their full time to governing. Give everyone what you owe him: If your owe taxes, pay taxes; if revenue, then revenue; if respect, then respect; if honor, then honor. Rom. 13:5–7

I urge, then, first of all, that requests, prayers, intercession
and thanksgiving be made for everyone—for kings
and all those in authority, that we may live peaceful
and quiet lives in all godliness and holiness. This is
good, and pleases God our Savior. 1 Tim. 2:1–3

Remind the people to be subject to rulers and authorities, to
be obedient, to be ready to do whatever is good. Titus 3:1

Submit yourselves for the Lord's sake to every authority instituted
among men: whether to the king, as the supreme authority,
or to governors, who are sent by him to punish those who do
wrong and to commend those who do right. 1 Peter 2:13–14

Almighty and everlasting Father, You are the source of all authority so that those who bear the sword wield it as Your servants and with accountability to You. Give us the wisdom to recognize this and so live decent and peaceable lives, praying for those in public office, honoring them in word and deed, and gladly rendering to them what is theirs even as we render to You that which is Yours alone; through Jesus Christ, our Lord. Amen.

This section of the Table of Duties gives expression to the teaching of the "two kingdoms" or "two governments" of God. God is governing both kingdoms but by different means and toward different ends.

Although Luther treats government prior to family in the Table of Duties, for the reformer the political order was founded on the household because "all other authority is derived and developed out of the authority of parents."[8] After the fall, there is a necessity to this estate in Luther's thinking, for it functions as a coercive means to prevent human society from collapsing into complete chaos and corruption:

> There was no government of the state before sin, for there was no need of it. Civil government is a remedy required by our corrupted nature. It is necessary that lust be held in check by the bonds of the laws and by penalties.[9]

Government, according to Luther, was established in creation out of the household, but the state is established after the fall.

Temporal authority is clearly established by God, and Luther points to Genesis 9:6 ("Whoever sheds the blood of man, by man shall his blood be shed") as proof for this in his treatise *Temporal Authority*.[10] The temporal offices of human government are put in place by God to restrain evildoers. Luther asserts that it

---

8 LC I 141; K-W 405.

9 *Lectures on Genesis* (1535–45/1544–54), AE 1:104.

10 *Temporal Authority* (1523), AE 45:86.

is necessary to separate all children of Adam into two groups: those who belong to the kingdom of God (all true believers in Christ) and those who belong to the kingdom of this world. He writes that "if all the world were composed of real Christians, that is, true believers, there would be no need for or benefits from prince, king, lord, sword, or law."[11] However, such is not reality in this fallen world. For this reason, God has

> ordained two governments: the spiritual, by which the Holy Spirit produces Christians and righteous people under Christ; and the temporal, which restrains the un-Christian and wicked.[12]

Both governments must remain, but we must carefully distinguish between the two.

"No one can become righteous in the sight of God by means of the temporal government, without Christ's spiritual government."[13] Christians are righteous through faith in Christ. Thus they do not need temporal government for their own sake.

> Since a true Christian lives and labors on earth not for himself alone but for his neighbor, he does by the very nature of his spirit even what he himself has no need of, but is needful and useful to his neighbor. Because the sword is most beneficial and necessary for the whole world in order to preserve peace, punish sin, and restrain the wicked, the Christian submits most willingly to the rule of the sword, pays his taxes, honors those in authority, serves, helps, and does all he can to assist the governing authority, that it may continue to function and be held in honor and fear. Although he has no need of these things for himself—to him they are not essential—nevertheless, he concerns himself about what is serviceable and of benefit to others, as Paul teaches in Ephesians 5 [:21–6:9].[14]

The Christian lives in God's kingdom inwardly and in the world's kingdom outwardly.

---

11   *Temporal Authority* (1523), AE 45:89.

12   *Temporal Authority* (1523), AE 45:91.

13   *Temporal Authority* (1523), AE 45:92.

14   *Temporal Authority* (1523), AE 45:94.

Christ himself made this distinction, and summed it all up very nicely when he said in Matthew 22 [:21], "Render to Caesar the things that are Caesar's and to God the things that are God's." Now, if the imperial power extended into God's kingdom and authority, and were not something separate, Christ would not have made this distinction. For, as has been said, the soul is not under the authority of Caesar; he can neither teach nor guide it, neither kill it nor give it life, neither bind it nor loose it, neither judge it nor condemn it, neither hold it fast nor release it. All this he would have to do, had he the authority to command it and to impose laws upon it. But with respect to the body, property, and honor he has indeed to do these things, for such matters are under his authority.[15]

Gerhard Ebeling nicely summarizes Luther's stance as it is reflected in the Table of Duties: "Caesar must be given no less, but no more either, than what is Caesar's."[16]

∽०੮੭०∽

To Husbands

Husbands, in the same way be considerate as you live with
your wives, and treat them with respect as the weaker
partner and as heirs with you of the gracious gift of life,
so that nothing will hinder your prayers. 1 Peter 3:7

Husbands, love your wives and do not
be harsh with them. Col. 3:19

To Wives

Wives, submit to your husbands as to the Lord. Eph. 5:22

They were submissive to their own husbands, like Sarah, who
obeyed Abraham and called him her master. You are her daughters
if you do what is right and do not give way to fear. 1 Peter 3:5–6

---

15 *Temporal Authority* (1523), AE 45:111.

16 Gerhard Ebeling, *Luther: An Introduction to His Thought*, trans. R. A. Wilson (Philadelphia: Fortress, 1972), 403.

To Parents

Fathers, do not exasperate your children; instead, bring them up in the training and instruction of the Lord. Eph. 6:4

To Children

Children, obey your parents in the Lord, for this is right. "Honor your father and your mother"—which is the first commandment with a promise—"that it may go well with you and that you may enjoy long life on the earth." Eph. 6:1–3

To Workers of All Kinds

Slaves, obey your earthly masters with respect and fear, and with sincerity of heart, just as you would obey Christ. Obey them not only to win their favor when their eye is on you, but like slaves of Christ, doing the will of God from your heart. Serve wholeheartedly, as if you were serving the Lord, not men, because you know that the Lord will reward everyone for whatever good he does, whether he is slave or free. Eph. 6:5–8

To Employers and Supervisors

Masters, treat your slaves in the same way. Do not threaten them, since you know that He who is both their Master and yours is in heaven, and there is no favoritism with Him. Eph. 6:9

To Youth

Young men, in the same way be submissive to those who are older. All of you, clothe yourselves with humility toward one another, because, "God opposes the proud but gives grace to the humble." Humble yourselves, therefore, under God's mighty hand, that He may lift you up in due time. 1 Peter 5:5–6

To Widows

The widow who is really in need and left all alone puts her hope in God and continues night and day to pray and to ask God for help. But the widow who lives for pleasure is dead even while she lives. 1 Tim. 5:5–6

To Everyone

The commandments . . . are summed up in this one
rule: "Love your neighbor as yourself." Rom. 13:9

I urge . . . that requests, prayers, intercession and
thanksgiving be made for everyone. 1 Tim. 2:1

**Merciful Father, You have set the solitary in families where we may love
and serve one another. We give You thanks for the gift of marriage and family.
Grant that husbands and wives honor and cherish each other in lifelong fidelity. Give children the wisdom to obey their parents that it may go well with
them and that they may enjoy a long life on the earth. Bless each in his or her
daily work; through Jesus Christ, our Lord. Amen.**

"Life within the family is not a requirement but a fact, an existential situation."[17] "Household" is inclusive not only of the nuclear family but also of all those
who live and work under the same roof. Marriage is at the center of this estate, for
it is through this lifelong union of man and woman that God creates and nurtures
new human life. This is the place where daily bread is given and received. Living
before the Industrial Revolution (after which daily work is generally separated
from the home), Luther saw work in the context of the family and for the good
of those people who are the nearest neighbors.

Fundamental for the household is God's institution of marriage.[18] In divesting
marriage of its sacramental status, Luther actually elevates marriage as he makes
it equal or superior to celibacy. Carter Lindberg observes:

---

17   Werner Elert, *Christian Ethos*, 81.

18   Here see Oswald Bayer, "Luther's View of Marriage," in *Freedom in Response: Lutheran Ethics:
Sources and Controversies*, trans. Jeffrey Cayzer (Oxford: Oxford University Press, 2007). Bayer notes: "In
the light of all this, we can understand why Luther placed so much emphasis on the 'estate' of marriage.
For us this has become an old-fashioned word that suggests something solid and immovable. But for
Luther the concept of estate was intimately connected with both steadfastness and energy, products of the
reliability of the Word that ensures that life together will have the quality of endurance. The Word holds
all the various facets of an active life together, its beauty and peace as well as its crises and conflicts. The
Word of God lends stability to the estate of marriage and brings about the unconditional and permanent
unity of one man and one woman" (170).

Luther's application of evangelical theology to marriage and family desacramentalized marriage; desacralized the clergy and resacralized the life of the laity; opposed the maze of canonical impediments to marriage; strove to unravel the skein of canon law, imperial law, and German customs; and joyfully affirmed God's good creation, including sexual relations.[19]

In the Table of Duties, Luther attends to the God-given responsibilities of both husband and wife.

Husbands are exhorted to love and be considerate toward their wives on the basis of 1 Peter 3:7. Physically, the wife is the weaker partner, but spiritually she is bound with him in the common calling to faith and the inheritance of the gift of life in Christ. This is a union that is to be tended and guarded so that the life of prayer is unimpeded.[20]

God's ordering of marriage is not arbitrary. Husbands are to love their wives as the heavenly Bridegroom loves His Bride, the Church (Colossians 3:19), and wives are to submit to their husbands as the Church yields to Christ (Ephesians 5:22).[21]

Parents are God's masks through which He bestows human life. They are also His representatives who guard and govern the lives of children entrusted to their care.[22] The Table of Duties addresses both parents and children. Hans Schwarz observes:

19   Carter Lindberg, "The Future of a Tradition: Luther and the Family," in *All Theology Is Christology: Essays in Honor of David P. Scaer*, ed. Dean Wenthe et al. (Fort Wayne, IN: Concordia Theological Seminary Press, 2000), 133. Also see Michael Parsons, *Reformation Marriage: The Husband and Wife Relationship in the Theology of Luther and Calvin* (Edinburgh: Rutherford House, 2005), 103–212; and William Lazareth, *Luther on the Christian Home* (Philadelphia: Muhlenberg Press, 1960).

20   Here see also Leonhard Goppelt, *A Commentary on 1 Peter*, trans. John E. Alsup (Grand Rapids: Eerdmans, 1993), 226–28. Goppelt notes that " 'your prayers' are certainly not those of the husbands alone, but the common prayers of husband and wife. Jesus himself taught that prayer is impeded when a relationship with a fellow human being is troubled. Whenever the most intimate human relationship—marriage—is not lived out satisfactorily the prayers of those involved are 'hindered'; they do not achieve the proper stature and do not reach oneness with God's will and provision" (*Commentary on 1 Peter*, 228).

21   Here see the extended treatment by Thomas Winger, "The Gospel in God's Order: The Bridegroom and the Bride," in *Ephesians*, Concordia Commentary (St. Louis: Concordia, 2015), 598–653.

22   Here note Paul Althaus: "Luther particularly emphasizes the authority of parents. Parents stand 'in the place of God.' They have the highest authority on earth. All other human authority—for example, the authority of the secular government—is derived from parental authority. Parental authority is uniquely different from all other authority for it functions in both governments. Parents not only exercise authority over their children in secular government, but they also proclaim the gospel to their children. Thus they are at one and the same time secular authorities and, through the universal priesthood, spiritual author-

Children should see their parents as representing God. Hence Luther wrote in his *Small Catechism* that we should "Honor, serve, obey, love, and respect" our parents. These five verbs belong together since to honor someone cannot be without love and respect. All this is not natural but requires a certain degree of obedience. Parents are the highest unified authority that their children initially know. Their authority, however, is not grounded in any parental claim to power but finds its limits in the divine commission of parents for the children God has entrusted to them.[23]

Parents are not to make it difficult for children to obey the Fourth Commandment through unnecessary harshness that would exasperate their offspring. Rather, it is given to the parental office to bring up children in the discipline and instruction of the Lord (Ephesians 6:4). Redemption does not exempt children from obedience to parents, as there is a temporal benefit attached to the Fourth Commandment that is reaffirmed by Paul as he cites the language of the Old Testament: "that it may go well with you and that you may live long in the land" (Ephesians 6:3).[24]

In the sixteenth century, work[25] was largely done in the context of the family, so Luther includes "workers of all kinds" and "employers and supervisors" along with "youth" and "widows" within the domestic order. Workers perform their jobs as people who are under the Lord's supervision, laboring not to please earthly masters but Christ (Ephesians 6:5–8). Earthly masters and employers are to exercise their authority with the realization that they also are under a heavenly Lord who shows no favoritism (Ephesians 6:9). Youth are to live in humility (1 Peter 5:5–6), while widows are to put their hope in God, praying "night and day" so as not to live for pleasure (1 Timothy 5:3–16).

In language reminiscent of the *Confession concerning Christ's Supper* written in the previous year, Luther concludes this section of the Small Catechism with texts from Romans 13:9, which calls for the Christian to love the neighbor as he

---

ities for their children" (*The Ethics of Martin Luther*, trans. Robert C. Schultz [Philadelphia: Fortress, 1972], 99).

23   Hans Schwarz, *The Human Being: A Theological Anthropology* (Grand Rapids: Eerdmans, 2013), 330.

24   See Thomas Winger, "Order 'in the Lord': Parents/Children, Masters/Slaves," in *Ephesians*, Concordia Commentary (St. Louis: Concordia, 2015), 654–96.

25   For a helpful summary of Luther's understanding of work, see Althaus, *Ethics of Martin Luther*, 101–4.

or she loves self, and 1 Timothy 2:1, which urges prayers for all people. In this way, Luther concludes the catechism as a handbook for Christian life and prayer, a pattern of sound words for faith and love, demonstrating that "the place where the two kingdoms are held together is the calling."[26]

---

26   Leif Grane, *The Augsburg Confession: A Commentary*, trans. John Rasmussen (Minneapolis: Augsburg, 1987), 174.

Appendices

Appendix I: The Catechism as the Handbook for the Vocation of the Laity in Worship and Prayer[1]

This essay endeavors to demonstrate that Luther's Small Catechism was not only a handbook of Christian doctrine, but a book of prayer and life. As such, the catechism is especially geared to the laity, tutoring them in how to receive God's gifts in the Divine Service and how to call upon His name in prayer, praise, and thanksgiving.

Einar Billing has helpfully described the rhythm of the Christian life as a movement from the forgiveness of sins to one's calling in the world and from the place of the calling back to the forgiveness of sins.[2] In a similar fashion, Jonathan Trigg speaks of the circularity of the Christian life in Luther's baptismal theology as the Christian is always returned to baptism.[3] With the descriptions of both Billing and Trigg, we see something of the dynamic operative in the catechism's framing of prayer and vocation. Every Lutheran layperson confesses the Small Catechism in his confirmation. If we are to examine the vocation of the laity in worship and prayer, we are best served in turning to the catechism itself, for the catechism as envisioned by Luther was not only a summation of doctrinal instruction but also a book to tutor the believer in prayer and in the Christian's calling to faith in Christ and life in the world. As the formulators of the Formula of Concord put it:

> And because these matters also concern the laity and the salvation of their souls, we pledge ourselves also to the Small and Large Catechisms of Dr. Luther, as both catechisms are found in Luther's printed works, as a Bible of the Laity, in which everything is summarized that is treated in detail in Holy Scripture and that is necessary for a Christian to know for salvation [Ep. para. 5].

---

1   "The Catechism as the Handbook for the Vocation of the Laity in Worship and Prayer" was originally presented at the Pieper Lectures at Concordia Seminary, St. Louis, Mo., in 2006, then published in *The Lutheran Doctrine of Vocation*, ed. John A. Maxfield (St. Louis: Concordia Historical Institute and Luther Academy, 2008), 81–97.

2   Einar Billing, *Our Calling*, trans. Carl Rasmussen (Philadelphia: Fortress, 1964), 38.

3   Jonathan Trigg, *Baptism in the Theology of Martin Luther* (Boston: Brill Academic Publishers, 2001), 169ff.

The structure of the first three chief parts of the catechism moves toward prayer. The command of the Decalogue is brought together with the promise of the Creed in Luther's explanation of the conclusion of the Lord's Prayer: "That I should be certain that such petitions are acceptable to and heard by our Father in heaven, for he himself *commanded* us to pray like this and has *promised* to hear us" (SC III.21; emphasis added).

To fear, love, and trust in God above all things is to hallow His name, that is, "to use that very name in every time of need to call on, pray to, praise and give thanks to God" (SC I.4). The Decalogue itself establishes the agenda for our praying as it unveils the neediness of our creaturely existence in a world of sin, death, and the devil.[4] The Creed narrates the generosity of the triune God toward His creatures. Oswald Bayer sees in Luther's usage of the words "without any merit and worthiness in me" in his explanation of the First Article a confession of justification by faith alone in relation to creation.[5] All that we are and all that we have comes from God alone.

After confessing the gifts of God in creation, Luther concludes, "For all this I owe it to God to thank and praise, serve and obey him" (SC II.355). Luther will return to this theme at the end of the catechism as he appends the daily prayers and Table of Duties to the Six Chief Parts. We thank and praise God in the morning when we rise from sleep and in the evening when we retire to sleep and as we sit down to eat. On these daily occasions when our lack of autonomy is most evident, we praise and thank God. These are times for praying the catechism as Luther instructs us to pray the Creed and the Our Father morning and evening, to sing the hymn on the Ten Commandments as we go to our labor, and to pray the Lord's Prayer as a table prayer. Luther's use of the Creed and the Lord's Prayer, texts associated with the liturgy of Holy Baptism, demonstrates the character of "the baptismal spirituality" of the catechism, as one writer has put it.[6] We might also observe here how the morning and evening prayer pick up themes from the Our Father, thus echoing the catechism. Prayer for Luther does not lead to withdrawal from the world but rather to life in the world, the life of vocation within the structures of creation. God is served and obeyed within

4   For a masterful exposition of this point see James Nestingen, "The Lord's Prayer in Luther's Catechism," *Word & World* 22 (Winter 2002): 36–48.

5   Oswald Bayer, "I Believe That God Has Created Me with All That Exists. An Example of Catechetical-Systematics," *Lutheran Quarterly* VIII (Summer 1994): 137.

6   Glen Borreson, "Luther's Morning and Evening Prayer as Baptismal Spirituality," *Word & World* 22 (Winter 2002): 60.

His creation—in congregation, civil government, home, and workplace. These are the masks behind which God serves us and receives our service born of faith.

James Nestingen observes that by way of the Small Catechism Luther "moved the village altar into the family kitchen, literally bringing instruction in the faith home to the intimacies of family life."[7] Luther recasts traditional monastic prayer forms in an evangelical way. Luther uses liturgical practices of the tradition such as the trinitarian name, the sign of the cross, and the literary elements of the prayer offices, but he recasts these items in the context of daily life.[8] As Dorothea Wendebourg notes:

> In the Small Catechism . . . we find a short order for morning and evening prayer, the "blessing for the morning" (*Morgensegen*) and the "blessing for the evening" (*Abendsegen*). These prayers are designed to mark the spiritual beginning and end of each day for the whole family. They combine the Lord's Prayer, the Creed, and a hymn: a small breviary for the Christian household. The idea is undeniably monastic, and of monastic origin are especially those parts that form the center of the short liturgy: the blessings for morning and evening. The former had been a traditional monastic morning blessing, now used by Luther, with only slight alterations, as the standard morning prayer for the "world," with a parallel version made up for the evening.[9]

---

7   James Nestingen, *Martin Luther: A Life* (Minneapolis: Augsburg Fortress, 2005), 76.

8   See Albrecht Peters, *Kommentar zu Luthers Katechismen*, vol. 5 (Göttingen: Vandenhoeck & Ruprecht, 1994), 191–204. See also Charles Arand, *That I May Be His Own: An Overview of Luther's Catechism* (St. Louis: Concordia Publishing House, 2000), 67–70; Borreson, "Luther's Morning and Evening Prayer," 55–63; and William R. Russell, *Praying for Reform* (Minneapolis: Augsburg Fortress, 2005), 13–23.

9   Dorothea Wendebourg, "Luther on Monasticism," *Lutheran Quarterly* (Summer 2005): 140. In a footnote Wendebourg describes how Luther used this traditional monastic material in an evangelical way: "The original prayer came from a Latin collection of late medieval texts and spiritual instructions by the Dutchman Johannes Mauburnus (d. 1501/1502). Here, too, it was combined with other liturgical elements, of which Luther kept only the first, an invocation of the Trinity together with the sign of the cross (in Mauburnus the invocation was Christological, followed by the above-mentioned prayer, a petition to the Blessed Virgin Mary asking her blessing, a psalm of praise and a hymn to the Virgin which referred to her as the source of our salvation and praise). In Luther's version the prayer is in German, therefore shorter and stylistically simpler than the original, but in other respects more specific. E.g., Luther gives thanks for 'protection during the night from all perils and dangers' (where Mauburnus has only a general thanksgiving for protection at night), he asks for protection from 'all sin and evil, that my entire life and work please thee' (where Mauburnus asks that 'my service [*servitus*] may be pleasing to thee'). Luther also added a formula of commitment which entrusts one's whole life to God, and a plea for protection by God's guardian angel" (149–50).

The catechism functions to tutor the believer in genuine prayer through its catechesis of the Lord's Prayer and to give form to the voice of faith within the daily cycle of life—getting out of bed and going to bed and mealtime. Prayer is not a retreat from the world; prayer is embedded within the fabric of creaturely life. For Luther, Walther von Loewenich says, "Prayer is not a little garden of Paradise, where the one weary of the Word of the cross might take a little rest, but prayer is just the battleground where the sign of the cross has been raised."[10]

Luther's preparation of the catechism was the culmination of over a decade of pastoral work aimed at equipping the believer for a life of prayer and vocation. Along with his catechetical sermons, the *Personal Prayer Book* (*Betbüchlein*) of 1522 would become a tributary flowing into the catechism. With the advent of the printing press, prayer books became more elaborate and more accessible to the laity. These late medieval prayer books included catalogues of virtues and vices to be used in preparation for confession, explanation of the steps necessary for salvation, prayers for various times and occasions, meditative prayers on the passion of Christ, prayers to the saints, and the penitential psalms. These books shaped the piety of laypeople at the grassroots level. Luther's *Personal Prayer Book* was an attempt to provide an evangelical alternative to these manuals using biblical material. Luther notes the need for a reformation of prayer books:

> I regard the personal prayer books as by no means the least objec-
> tionable. They drub into the minds of simple people such a wretched
> counting up of sins and going to confession, such un-Christian
> tomfoolery about prayers to God and his saints! Moreover, these
> books are puffed up with promises of indulgences and come out
> with decorations in red ink and pretty titles. . . . These books need
> a basic and thorough reformation if not total extermination.[11]

Luther would use the Ten Commandments, the Creed, and the Lord's Prayer as the core texts for Christian praying. The *Personal Prayer Book* reflects Luther's growing understanding of the necessity for brevity and clarity in catechetical forms:

---

10   Walther von Loewenich, *Luther's Theology of the Cross,* trans. Herbert J. A. Bouman (Minneapolis: Augsburg Publishing House, 1976), 143. Also Nestingen ("Lord's Prayer in Luther's Catechism," 37): "As Luther heard it (the Lord's Prayer) there, teaching the faithful to pray, the Lord Jesus is at the same time telling believers what to expect in the crucible of everyday life, where the heart is contended for by the powers at work in this age—the devil, the world, and the sinful self—as well as the Spirit of the new age, released in Christ's death and resurrection. Thus for Luther, the Lord's Prayer is a continuing lesson in the theology of the cross."

11   AE 43:11–12.

Indeed, the total content of Scripture and preaching and everything a Christian needs to know is quite fully and adequately comprehended in these three items (Ten Commandments, Creed, Lord's Prayer). They summarize everything with such brevity and clarity that no one can complain or make any excuse that the things necessary for his salvation are too complicated or difficult for him to remember.[12]

Luther describes his approach:

Three things a person must know in order to be saved. First, he must know what to do and what to leave undone. Second, when he realizes that he cannot measure up to what he should do or leave undone, he needs to know where to go to find the strength that he requires. Third, he must know how to seek and obtain that strength. It is just like a sick person who first has to determine the nature of his sickness, then find out what to do or leave undone. After that he has to know where to get the medicine which will help him do or leave undone what is right for a healthy person. Then he has to desire or search for this medicine and to obtain it or have it brought to him. Thus the commandments teach man to recognize his sickness, enabling him to perceive what he must do or refrain from doing, consent to or refuse, and so he will recognize himself to be a sinful and wicked person. The Creed will teach and show him where to find medicine—grace—which will help him to become devout and keep the commandments. The Creed points him to God and his mercy, given and made plain to him in Christ. Finally, the Lord's Prayer teaches all this, namely, through the fulfillment of God's commandments everything will be given to him. In these three are the essentials of the entire Bible.[13]

The *Personal Prayer Book* provides an overview of the Ten Commandments. The first table of the law (the right-hand tablet) instructs us in our duty to God inwardly (faith) and outwardly (God's name and worship). The second table of the law (the left-hand tablet) teaches us our obligation to the neighbor. Then Luther provides instruction in how each commandment is broken or fulfilled in the way of a *Beichtspiegel* or "mirror for confession." For example, the First Com-

---

12 AE 43:13.

13 AE 43:13–14.

mandment is violated by superstition, failure to trust and rely on God's mercy at all times, every kind of doubt, despair, and false belief. On the other hand, this commandment is fulfilled by the "fear and love of God in true faith, at all times, firmly trusting him in all that he does, accepting in simple, quiet confidence, everything whether good or bad."[14]

As the gospel follows the law, Luther moves from the Decalogue to the baptismal creed.[15] The threefold division of the Creed is reflective of the doctrine of the Trinity. Faith is defined both as knowing and trusting in the one true God. Living faith is connected with the First Commandment: "Only a faith that ventures everything in life and in death on what is said (in Scripture) of God makes a person a Christian and obtains all he desires from God. No corrupt or hypocritical heart can have such a faith; this is a living faith as the First Commandment demands: I am your God; you shall have no other gods."[16]

The First Article renounces every idolatry and false belief. Trust is located only in God: "I take the risk of placing my confidence only in the one, invisible, inscrutable, and only God, who created heaven and earth and who alone is superior to all creation. Again, I am not terrified by all the wickedness of the devil and his cohorts because God is superior to them all." This trust is steadfast in spite of everything that contradicts it: "I trust in him steadfastly, no matter how long he may delay, prescribing neither a goal, nor a time, nor a measure, nor a way (for God to respond to me), but leaving all to his divine will in a free, honest, and genuine faith. If he is almighty, what could I lack that God could not give or do for me?"[17] The Second Article unfolds the confession that Jesus is the one true Son of God, begotten from all eternity and made man to suffer, die, and rise again for our salvation. Biblical texts are used to unpack each phrase of the Second Article. The Third Article sets forth the work of the Holy Spirit. Here Luther focuses on the forgiveness of sins for Christ's sake in the context of the church as that community created and sustained by the Word of forgiveness preached and bestowed in the sacraments.

If the Creed is the summation of God's Word to us in the trinitarian gospel, then the Lord's Prayer gives voice to the faith created by that Word. Luther's exposition of the Lord's Prayer comes by way of prayers that are derived from

---

14   AE 43:22.

15   On the law/gospel distinction in Luther's catechetical work, see Dennis Ngien, "Theology and Practice of Prayer in Luther's Devotional and Catechetical Writings," *Luther-Bulletin* 14 (2005): 44–65.

16   AE 43:23–24.

17   AE 43:25.

each petition. "Our Father" is a cry for faith that we may remain God's children rather than become His enemies. Themes of childlike certainty and comforting trust in God's fatherly mercy emerge. "Hallowed be thy name" is a prayer for protection from all that would bring dishonor to God's name. "May thy kingdom come near" is a petition for the success of God's Word against "unbelief, despair, and from boundless envy." "Thy will be done equally in heaven and earth" is a prayer for mercy. "Therefore have mercy upon us, O dear Father, and let nothing happen just because it is our own will." "Give us this day our daily bread" calls upon the Father "that the life, words, deeds, and sufferings of Christ be preached, made known, and preserved for us and all the world." Luther paraphrases the Fifth Petition as "And do not hold us accountable for debts, as we do not hold our debtors accountable," taking it as a supplication for the forgiveness of sins. "In this petition belong all psalms and prayers which invoke God's mercy for our sin." "And lead us not into temptation" is a prayer against the flesh, the world, and the devil. "But deliver us from evil" is a prayer for the final accomplishment of the Father's holy will—eschatological deliverance. Amen is the signature of faith that lays hold to all of God's promises in Christ.[18]

Eric Gritsch asserts that "Luther saw the beginning of catechetical instruction as an initiation to worship."[19] In the Preface to the German Mass of 1526, Luther calls for the liturgical usage of the catechetical core of the Decalogue, Creed, and Lord's Prayer, even giving examples of how such catechization might take place. He asserts that "the German service needs a plain and simple, fair and square catechism" so that worshipers might know the Ten Commandments, the Creed, and the Lord's Prayer.[20] There is interplay between the catechization that takes place in the divine service and the catechesis that Christian parents are to provide in the home, anticipating Luther's introduction to each of the chief parts of the catechism: "As the head of the family should teach them in a simple way to his household." In the German Mass, Luther inserts a catechetical paraphrase of the Lord's Prayer after the sermon and in anticipation of the Lord's Supper. This exposition, a substitute for the *sursum corda*, serves as an admonition to the repentant and faithful reception of Christ's testament, and as a way of teaching Christian prayer. Even a quick reading of the paraphrase reveals its literary and theological commonality with the treatment of the Our Father in the Small Catechism.

---

18   AE 43:29, 32–33, 37.

19   Eric Gritsch, "Luther's Catechisms of 1529: Whetstones of the Church," *Lutheran Theological Seminary Bulletin* 60 (1980): 4.

20   AE 53:61–68; quote at p. 64.

The catechism would become a compass to navigate the believer in the true worship of God, that is, worship which looks to God alone for every good and trusts in Him alone for the forgiveness of sins. The assessment of Vilmos Vajta is correct: "The First Commandment is basic for Luther's idea of worship; for faith is the fulfillment of the First Commandment, and idolatry is nothing but unbelief."[21] Luther's exposition of the First Commandment in the Large Catechism bears this out. After Luther defines a god as that person or thing in which we "look for all good and in which we are to find refuge in all need" (LC I.2), he explains that idolatry can be either of a creaturely or spiritual variety. There are the idolatries of mammon: "Those who have money and property feel secure, happy, and fearless, as if they were sitting in the midst of paradise. On the other hand, those who have nothing doubt and despair as if they knew of no god at all" (LC I.6–8). Then there is spiritual idolatry that is rooted in the trust of one's own cultic works, such as the invocation of the saints:

> There is, moreover, another false worship. This is the greatest idolatry that we have practiced up to now, and it is still rampant in the world. All the religious orders are founded upon it. It involves only that conscience that seeks help, comfort, and salvation in its own works and presumes to wrest heaven from God. It keeps track of how often it has made endowments, fasted, celebrated Mass, etc. It relies on such things and boasts of them, unwilling to receive anything as a gift of God, but desiring to earn everything by itself or to merit everything by works of supererogation, just as if God were in our service or debt and we were his liege lords. What is this but to have made God into an idol—indeed, an "apple god"—and to have set ourselves up as God? [LC I.22–23]

The catechetical exposition of the First Commandment orients the believer's life away from his own works or merits to the work of God so that he is tutored in the receptivity of faith.

The Second Commandment, like the First Petition of the Lord's Prayer, guides the life of worship and prayer as God's name is not to be used to curse, swear, practice magic, lie, or deceive but to be called upon in prayer, praise, and thanksgiving. As with the other commandments, the Second Commandment is anchored in the First Commandment. Luther makes this connection explicit: "In

---

21   Vilmos Vajta, *Luther on Worship: An Introduction,* trans. U. S. Leupold (Philadelphia: Muhlenberg Press, 1958), 3.

the Second Commandment we are told to fear God and not take his name in vain by cursing, lying, deceiving, and other kinds of corruption and wickedness, but to use his name properly by calling upon him in prayer, praise, and thanksgiving, that spring from that love and trust that the First Commandment requires" (LC I.326).

This theme of the First Commandment is furthered in Luther's exposition of the Third Commandment. The command to "hallow the day of rest" (LC I.78) is not interpreted by Luther in the sense of keeping a day free from secular pursuits.

> As far as outward observance is concerned, the commandment was given to the Jews alone. . . . Therefore, according to its outward meaning, this commandment does not concern us Christians. It is an entirely external matter, like other regulations of the Old Testament associated with particular customs, persons, times and places, from all of which we are set free through Christ [LC I.80, 82].[22]

In his catechism hymn on the Decalogue, "These Are the Holy Ten Commands," written in 1524, Luther gives doxological expression that will be unfolded in both the Small and the Large Catechism:

> **"You shall observe the worship day**
> **That peace may fill your home, and pray,**
> **And put aside the work you do,**
> **So that God may work in you."**
> **Have mercy, Lord!** (*LSB* 581:4)

Vajta writes:

> In no sense is this worship a preparatory stage which faith could ultimately leave behind. Rather faith might be defined as a passive cult (*cultus passivus*) because in this life it will always depend on the worship which God imparts Himself—a gift granted to the believing congregation. This is confirmed in Luther's Explanation of the Third Commandment. To him Sabbath rest means more than a pause from work. It should be an opportunity for God to do his work on man. God wants to distract man from his daily toil and so open him to God's gifts. To observe the Sabbath is not a good work

---

22   Also see Luther's *How Christians Should Regard Moses* (AE 35:155–74); and Heinrich Bornkamm, *How Christians Should Regard Moses,* trans. Eric W. and Ruth C. Gritsch (Philadelphia: Fortress, 1969), 121–23.

which man could offer to God. On the contrary, it means pausing, letting God do His work in us and for us. . . . Thus Luther's picture of the Sabbath is marked by the passivity of man and the activity of God. And it applies not only to certain holy days on the calendar, but to the Christian life in its entirety, testifying to man's existence as a creature of God who waits by faith for the life of the world to come. Through God's activity in Christ, man is drawn into the death and resurrection of the Redeemer and is so recreated a new man in Christ. The Third Commandment lays on us no obligation for specific works of any kind (not even spiritual or cultic works) but rather directs us to the work of God. And we do not come into contact with the latter except in the Service, where Christ meets us in the means of grace.[23]

In its treatment of the Third Commandment the catechism teaches the believer that the stance of faith is one of passivity before God. There is a place for works, but the location of good works is not in the church service but in the world, where the believer is enlivened to live by the gifts he has received in the Divine Service. The works commanded in the second table of the Decalogue come to fruition in the Table of Duties within the three estates of the congregation, civic government, and family.

But when it comes to salvation, it is the Lord who does the work. To the traditional catechetical core of the Ten Commandments, Creed, and Lord's Prayer Luther adds material on baptism, confession and absolution, and the Lord's Supper. Here Luther aims not only to teach the laity what baptism, confession and absolution, and the Lord's Supper are but also to teach them how to receive the gifts of Christ. Christians ought to know what the sacraments are but they should also know how to make salutary use of these gifts. So in his unfolding of baptism, Luther moves from the basic question, "What is baptism?" to the questions of baptism's benefits and work, to the final question concerning the significance of baptism for daily life. Luther breaks with the medieval devaluation of baptism to a rite of initiation, asserting the present tense promises of baptism for the Christian's ongoing struggle against sin. The inclusion of Luther's baptismal booklet of 1526 in many early editions of the Small Catechism functioned to teach Christian people the significance of baptism for their vocation to faith and life in Christ as is demonstrated by Luther's Preface.

---

23   Vajta, *Luther on Worship,* 130, 132.

In his treatment of confession, Luther provides not only catechetical instruction regarding the function of confession but also a liturgical template for Christians to use in confessing sin and receiving absolution from the pastor as from God Himself. Christians are taught how to identify and confess sin in the light of their vocation or "walk of life in light of the Ten Commandments" (SC V.20).

Luther's exposition of the Sacrament of the Altar sets forth the confession of Christ's body and blood over against both Roman Catholics and the Zwinglians.[24] Luther accents the gift character of the Lord's Supper as the basis for the salutary reception of the Sacrament. Thus Luther says that "fasting and bodily preparation are in fact a fine external discipline, but a person who has faith in these words, 'given for you' and 'shed for you for the forgiveness of sins,' is really worthy and well-prepared" (SC VI.9). Further evidence for Luther's aim of the catechism as preparation for Christians to receive Christ's gifts in the Lord's Supper can be seen in the Large Catechism: "All this is established from the words of Christ used to institute it (the Sacrament). So everyone who wishes to be a Christian and to go to the sacrament should know them. For we do not intend to admit to the sacrament and administer it to those who do not know what they seek or why they come" (LC V.2).

We have already noted that the Creed summarizes the work of the triune God for us in creation, redemption, and sanctification. The "this is most certainly true" at the end of each of the catechetical explanations forms the foundation for the catechism's exposition of the Lord's Prayer as Luther teaches that to call God "our Father" is to call upon Him as true children address their true father with boldness and confidence.

A further fruit of the Small Catechism in the life of prayer can be seen in Luther's celebrated letter to his friend, the Wittenberg barber Peter Beskendorf. Given the title *A Simple Way to Pray*, this tract of 1535 demonstrates how Luther uses the catechism to teach Christians how to pray. "Nowhere is the connection between order and freedom in Luther's practice so clearly seen as in his advice for Master Peter," says Martin Brecht.[25] Knowing that the flesh and the devil always attempt to impede the discipline of prayer, Luther writes:

> When I feel that I have become cool and joyless in prayer because of other thoughts (for the flesh and the devil always impede or obstruct prayer), I take my little psalter, hurry to my room, or, if it be the

---

24   See Arand, *That I May Be His Own,* 170–72.

25   Martin Brecht, *Martin Luther: The Preservation of the Church,* trans. James L. Schaaf (Minneapolis: Fortress, 1993), 14.

day and hour for it, to church where a congregation is assembled and, as time permits, I say quietly to myself and word-for-word the Ten Commandments, the Creed, and if I have time, some words of Christ or of Paul, or some psalms, just as a child might do.[26]

While Luther offers Peter a number of practical suggestions regarding the time and place of prayer, his focus is on the Lord's Prayer, the Ten Commandments, and to a lesser extent the Creed.

Luther gives a "model prayer" that serves as a preface to the Lord's Prayer. This prayer begins with a confession of unworthiness on account of sin, grounds prayer in the command and promise of God—echoing the Small Catechism—and implores the Father in the name of Jesus and in communion with "all thy saints and Christians on earth."[27] Each petition of Jesus' prayer is used as a foundation and platform for praying. Luther shows Peter how to unpack each petition for supplication and intercession. He provides model prayers as well as pastoral instruction along the way. For example, Luther inserts parenthetical admonition in regard to the person unable to forgive his neighbor under the Fifth Petition.

The great word of prayer is "Amen." It is the word of faith that binds us together with all Christians:

> Finally, mark this, that you must always speak the Amen firmly. Never doubt that God in his mercy will surely hear you and say "yes" to your prayers. Never think that you are kneeling or standing alone, rather think that the whole of Christendom, all devout Christians, are standing there beside you and you are standing among them in a common, united petition which God cannot disdain. Do not leave your prayer without having said or thought, "Very well, God has heard my prayer; this I know as a certainty and a truth." That is what Amen means.[28]

Praying the Lord's Prayer does not bind us to "words or syllables" but focuses attention on the thoughts comprehended therein.

> It may happen occasionally that I may get lost among so many ideas in one petition that I forgo the other six. If such an abundance of good thoughts comes to us we ought to disregard the other peti-

---

26   AE 43:193.

27   AE 43:194–95.

28   AE 43:198.

tions, make room for such thoughts, listen in silence, and under no circumstances obstruct them. The Holy Spirit himself preaches here, and one word of his sermon is far better than a thousand of our prayers. Many times I have learned more from one prayer than I might have learned from much reading and speculation.

Just as a barber has to pay attention to how he uses his razor, so must the Christian attend to prayer with "concentration and singleness of heart."[29] Luther concludes:

This in short is the way I use the Lord's Prayer when I pray it. To this day I suckle at the Lord's Prayer like a child, and as an old man eat and drink from it and never get my fill. It is the very best prayer, even better than the psalter, which is so very dear to me. It is surely evident that a real master composed and taught it. What a great pity that the prayer of such a master is prattled and chattered so irreverently all over the world! . . . In a word, the Lord's Prayer is the greatest martyr on earth (as are the name and word of God). Everybody tortures and abuses it; few take comfort and joy in its proper use.[30]

Reinhard Huetter has written recently of the "Lutheran eclipse"[31] of the Ten Commandments as a text for prayer and worship. Such a disappearance is not due to Luther.[32] Like the Lord's Prayer, the Ten Commandments are to be prayed. Luther suggests a fourfold template for praying the Ten Commandments:

I take one part after another and free myself as much as possible from distractions in order to pray. I divide each commandment into four parts, thereby fashioning a garland of four strands. That is, I think of each commandment as, first, instruction, which is really what it is intended to be, and consider what the Lord God demands

---

29   AE 43:199.

30   AE 43:200.

31   Reinhard Huetter, "The Ten Commandments as a Mirror of Sin(s): Anglican Decline, Lutheran Eclipse," *Pro Ecclesia* XIV (Winter 2005): 46–57.

32   See for example Luther's catechetical use of the Decalogue in the German Mass (AE 53:63–64). For the use of the catechism in Reformation orders see Charles Arand, "Catechismal Services: A Bridge Between Evangelism and Assimilation," *Concordia Journal* XXIII (July 1997): 177–200.

of me so earnestly. Second, I turn it into a thanksgiving; third, a confession; and fourth, a prayer.[33]

Luther then provides model prayers. For example, with the First Commandment Luther sees these four parts: 1) instruction: God teaches and expects us to have faith in no one or nothing other than God Himself; 2) thanksgiving: God is our God. He has provided us with all that we are and all that we have; 3) confession: We acknowledge our "countless acts of idolatry" and our ingratitude; and 4) prayer: Preserve us from unbelief and ingratitude.[34] In this way, Luther sees the Decalogue as providing multiple dimensions for prayer. He writes, "These are the Ten Commandments in their fourfold aspect, namely, as a school text, song book, penitential book, and prayer book. They are intended to help the heart come to itself and grow zealous in prayer."[35]

Luther concludes his instructions for Peter with "A Simple Exercise for Contemplating the Creed." Noting that the division of the Creed corresponds to the three persons of the Godhead, Luther invites Peter to consider each article in the light of God's work and our need. So we ponder the magnitude of God's gifts in creation, redemption, and sanctification while lamenting our lack of faith and gratitude.[36]

Luther's *A Simple Way to Pray* became something of a devotional classic. It demonstrated the application of Reformation theology to the life of Christians by providing an evangelical discipline for prayer and meditation shaped by common catechetical texts. William Russell writes:

> This document represents Luther's mature catechetical piety, the integration of theology and prayer in the context of catechesis. He shows here his long-standing attention to the practical concerns of the Christian life. His response to the question of his barber shows how the reformer viewed this kind of Reformation—believers living at the nexus of the Word of God, catechesis, and prayer. As a confessor of the faith, Luther recommends that believers "pray" the chief articles of the church's confession, that is "the Lay Bible," as found in the catechism.[37]

---

33 AE 43:200.

34 AE 43:200–201.

35 AE 43:209.

36 AE 43:209.

37 Russell, *Praying for Reform*, 71.

Frank Senn offers the opinion that "the reformers were concerned to train a cadre of preachers who would expound the scriptures, word by word, with recourse to the original languages," but they "did not take the next step of training congregations to listen to such sermons."[38] But is this really the case? The use of Luther's catechisms seems to suggest otherwise.[39] Certainly Luther's letter to the layman Peter is an example of how Luther himself trained the laity to use the catechism, and with such a use of the catechism one is prepared to listen to the Word of God as it is preached.

What does all of this mean for us today in our thinking about the life of worship and prayer in the vocation of the laity? I would offer a few observations growing out of what we have observed in Luther's catechetical work.

First, a sound doctrine of vocation will guard us from the activism that confuses our projects with God's work. Lutherans are rightly uncomfortable with the slogan made popular after the Second Vatican Council that "liturgy is the work of the people." Liturgy does not consist in our action but is the work of God who stoops down to give us gifts that we cannot obtain for ourselves. Does the passivity of the Lutheran definition leave no room for worship? Does not the Small Catechism bid us to "thank, praise, serve, and obey" God? If God serves us sacramentally, do we not also serve Him sacrificially?

For Luther, the distinction between faith and love is necessary both in liturgy and in vocation. In the liturgy, faith receives the gifts of Christ. In vocation, love gives to the neighbor even as Christ has given Himself to us. The distinction between faith and love lies behind the discussion of sacrifice in Article XXIV of the Apology. The Apology notes that there are two kinds of sacrifice. First of all, there is the atoning sacrifice, the sacrifice of propitiation whereby Christ made satisfaction for the sins of the world. This sacrifice has achieved reconciliation between God and humanity and so merits the forgiveness of sins. The other type of sacrifice is the eucharistic sacrifice. It does not merit forgiveness of sins, nor does it procure reconciliation with God, but it is rather a sacrifice of thanksgiving. According to Article XXIV of the Apology, eucharistic sacrifices include "the preaching of the gospel, faith, prayer, thanksgiving, confession, the affliction of the saints, indeed all the good works of the saints. These sacrifices are not satisfactions for those

---

38   Frank Senn, *The People's Work: A Social History of the Liturgy* (Minneapolis: Fortress, 2006), 193.

39   See Christopher Brown's work on the impact of catechetical hymnody (Christopher Boyd Brown, *Singing the Gospel: Lutheran Hymns and the Success of the Reformation* [Cambridge: Harvard University Press, 2005]); and Steven Ozment's analysis of the influence of catechetical instruction and preaching in the Reformation (Steven Ozment, *When Fathers Ruled: Family Life in Reformation Europe* [Cambridge: Harvard University Press, 1983]).

who offer them, nor can they be applied to others so as to merit the forgiveness of sins or reconciliation for others *ex opere operato*. They are performed by those who are already reconciled" (Ap. XXIV.24).

Spiritual sacrifices are rendered in the bodily life of the believer as his life is a channel of God's love and care for the neighbor in need. These sacrifices do not merit salvation or make a person righteous, but rather express love for the neighbor. God is not in need of our good works, but our neighbor is. Freed from the notion that he must make himself good in order to earn eternal life, the Christian is directed toward the neighbor's well-being. In *The Freedom of the Christian* Luther writes, "Although the Christian is thus free from all works, he ought in this liberty to empty himself, take upon himself the form of a servant, be made in the likeness of men, be found in human form, and to serve, help and in every way deal with his neighbor as he sees that God through Christ has dealt and still deals with him."[40]

Here the Christian is a *larva dei*, a mask of God, by which God gives daily bread to the inhabitants of the world. In this sense the Christian is a "little Christ" to his neighbor. Again in this treatise Luther writes: "Just as our neighbor is in need and lacks that in which we abound, so we were in need before God and lacked his mercy. Hence, as our heavenly Father has in Christ freely come to our aid, we also ought freely to help our neighbor through our body and its works, and each one become as it were a Christ to the other that we may be Christ to one another."[41] Just as Christ sacrificed Himself for us on the cross, we give ourselves sacrificially to the neighbor in love. This is expressed by Luther in the seventh of his "Invocavit sermons" preached at Wittenberg on 15 March 1522:

> We shall now speak of the fruit of this sacrament, which is love; that is, that we should treat our neighbor as God has treated us. Now we have received from God nothing but love and favor, for Christ has pledged and given us his righteousness and everything he has; he has poured out upon us all his treasures, which no man can measure and no angel can understand or fathom, for God is a glowing furnace of love, reaching even from the earth to the heavens. Love, I say, is a fruit of the sacrament.[42]

---

40   AE 31:366.
41   AE 31:367–68.
42   AE 51:95.

In his 1530 treatise *Admonition Concerning the Sacrament*, Luther makes a similar point: "Where such faith is thus continually refreshed and renewed, there the heart is also at the same time refreshed anew in its love of the neighbor and is made strong and equipped to do all good works and to resist sin and all temptations of the devil. Since faith cannot be idle, it must demonstrate the fruits of love by doing good and avoiding evil."[43]

Luther's teaching on the dual existence of the Christian in faith and love leads us to observe a connection with the teaching of the two governments or two kingdoms. Leif Grane points out that for Luther "the place where the two kingdoms are held together is the calling."[44] This calling is lived within the structures of creation. Luther identified these structures as the three "hierarchies" of "the ministry, marriage, and government."[45] It is within these structures of congregation, political order, and family life (which for Luther included the economic realm) that one exercises "the liturgy after the liturgy." The Christian does not seek to escape or withdraw from the world as in monasticism, but rather lives out his calling in the particular place where God has located him.

In his "Table of Duties" included in the Small Catechism, Luther identifies these duties as "holy orders" in an obvious play on words over against monastic teaching. Holy people do holy work. Sacrifice is re-located. No doubt Ernst Käsemann was influenced by the older liberalism that pitted "priestly religion" against "prophetic religion"; nevertheless he does echo a Lutheran theme in his exposition of Romans 12 as he states: "Christian worship does not consist of what is practiced at sacred sites, at sacred times, and with sacred acts (Schlatter). It is the offering of bodily existence in the otherwise profane sphere."[46] In a less polemic

---

43   AE 38:126.

44   Leif Grane, *The Augsburg Confession: A Commentary*, trans. John Rasmussen (Minneapolis: Augsburg Publishing House, 1987), 174.

45   On the significance of the three hierarchies or three orders, see Oswald Bayer, "Nature and Institution: Luther's Doctrine of the Three Orders," *Lutheran Quarterly* XII (Summer 1998): 125–60; and Knut Alfsvåg, "Christians in Society: Luther's Teaching on the Two Kingdoms and the Three Estates Today," *Logia: A Journal of Lutheran Theology* 14 (Reformation 2005): 15–20.

46   Ernst Käsemann, *Commentary on Romans* (Grand Rapids: Eerdmans, 1980), 329. Also note the comment of Paul Rorem: "Forgiven and renewed, we offer ourselves once again to God, not in mystery and ritual at the altar but in the gritty realities of the poor and the mission fields of our neighborhoods and work places." Paul Rorem, "The End of All Offertory Processions," *Dialog* (Fall 1996): 249. Luther speaks in the same way when in a 1527 letter to John Hess he describes how Christians are to go to the aid of the sick: "I know for certain that this work is pleasing to God and all angels when I do it in obedience to his will and as a divine service. . . . Godliness is nothing but divine service, and divine service is service to one's neighbor." Martin Luther, *Letters of Spiritual Counsel*, ed. Theodore Tappert (London: SCM Press, 1955), 238–39. Also note the remarks of Carl Wisløff: "We, not the Sacrament, are the sacrifice. But

tone, Carter Lindberg makes a similar point: "Daily work is a form of worship within the world (*weltlicher Gottesdienst*) through service to the neighbor."[47] The "thank, praise, serve, and obey" in the conclusion of the explanation of the First Article find their fulfillment in the daily prayers and Table of Duties.

The vocation of the laity is not to seek some sort of affirmation by imitating the clergy—this is actually a veiled form of clericalism. You are good for something in the church as you do what pastors ordinarily do! So it is thought that the laypeople are elevated, given a higher status if they have a role in liturgical leadership.[48] On the contrary, there is God-assigned dignity in living within the ordinary places of human life.

A few years ago the American church historian Mark Noll described Lutherans as "extraordinarily ordinary."[49] Observing that Lutherans unlike their Episcopalian and Presbyterian cousins have not made a name for themselves in American politics (no Lutheran has been elected to the presidency and only a handful of Lutherans serve as senators or governors) or in other more prominent places of public life, Noll probes to answer the question of the Lutheran difference. He concludes that Lutherans are "extraordinarily ordinary" and this is a good thing.

---

we live from the gifts of God's grace, that is, we are led through them from death to life. Sacrifice finds expression in just this. This event finds expression in worship through thanksgiving, praise, creed, and witness. But a true sacrifice is only this when it is consecrated through faith by daily walking in baptism, that is, walking in fear and faith, death and resurrection." Carl Wisløff, "Worship and Sacrifice," in *The Unity of the Church: A Symposium*, ed. Vilmos Vajta (Rock Island, Illinois: Augustana Book Concern, 1957), 164–65. Also Oswald Bayer: "Worship is first and last God's service to us, his sacrifice which took place for us, which he bestows in specific worship—'take and eat! I am here for you' (cf. 1 Cor. 11:24 with Gen. 2:16). This feature of worship is lost if we want to do as a work what we may receive as a gift." Oswald Bayer, "Worship and Theology," in *Worship and Ethics: Lutherans and Anglicans in Dialogue* (New York: Walther de Gruyter, 1996), 154.

47   Carter Lindberg, *Beyond Charity: Reformation Initiatives for the Poor* (Minneapolis: Fortress, 1993), 108.

48   A fictional letter from a mother to her daughter illustrates this point as the letter writer explains why she declined the pastor's invitation to serve as a lay reader: "They had a little dispute about who should read the Scripture lessons at Sunday services. It seems that some people want a chance to do it more often, while others are tired of hearing them read poorly. Pastor Haden, a true child of his time in matters liturgical, generally sides with the first group. Says he is just a minister to equip ministers. (I sometimes think the man was born uttering platitudes.) Although I don't want to make an issue of it, I myself never read the lessons. It's a form of a silent witness—maybe even protest. We have gradually begun to think of our 'ministry' as doing things in a church service. This, in fact, is what the liturgical renewal of the last few decades has largely amounted to. It is a revival of exactly what the Reformers turned away from in the 16th century—namely, the notion that only certain vocations are religious." Gilbert Meilaender, *Letters to Ellen* (Grand Rapids: Eerdmans, 1996), 91.

49   Mark Noll, "The Lutheran Difference," *First Things* 20 (February 1992): 31–40.

It is a fruit of the Lutheran understanding of vocation in the ordinary places of life—congregation and family, the workplace, and the community.

So when it comes to the life of the laity and the vocation of worship and prayer, it is life that is extraordinarily ordinary. It is a life that attends to the hearing of God's Word; receiving His sacraments; calling upon Him in prayer, praise, and thanksgiving; and then living in the world by engaging the tasks and bearing the cross that comes with those "holy orders" which are stations in worldly life.

Appendix II: Luther's Morning and Evening Prayers as Reflections of the Our Father

This chart was designed to show how the catechism's exposition of the Apostles' Creed and the Lord's Prayer flow into Luther's morning and evening prayers. Luther was immersed in the Psalms, so it is no surprise that phrases and images from the Psalms mesh with catechetical language in these prayers as is illustrated by the chart.

Morning Prayer	Evening Prayer	Our Father	Psalm
"I thank You, my heavenly Father, through Jesus Christ, Your dear Son"	same	"Our Father"	Psalm 138:1–2 Psalm 105:1 Psalm 118:1
"that You have kept me this night from all harm and danger"	"that You have graciously kept me this day"	"Give us this day our daily bread"	Psalm 5:3 Psalm 3:5 Psalm 88:13
"and I pray that You would keep me this day also from sin and every evil, that all my doings and life may please You"		"hallowed be Thy name, Thy kingdom come, Thy will be done"	Psalm 143:8 Psalm 25 Psalm 119:33–40
	"and I pray that You would forgive me all my sins where I have done wrong, and graciously keep me this night"	"and forgive us our trespasses as we forgive those who trespass against us; and lead us not into temptation"	Psalm 32 Psalm 130 Psalm 4:8 Psalm 121
"For into Your hands I commend myself, my body and soul, and all things. Let Your holy angel be with me, that the evil foe may have no power over me."	Same	"but deliver us from evil"	Psalm 31:5 Psalm 91:11
Amen	Amen	Amen	

Appendix III: The Psalms Organized According to the Lord's Prayer

Luther treasured the Psalter as that book of Holy Scriptures that painted the lives of the saints in living color, both at the height of joy and in the deep places of despair. Following Luther on this point, Dietrich Bonhoeffer suggested that the whole Psalter could be arranged according to the petitions of the Lord's Prayer.[1] This chart is an attempt to do just that.

Introduction:

Our Father who art in heaven.
Ps. 23, 42, 84, 116, 117, 118, 121, 131

(Remembrance of Baptism that gives us access to the Father)

First Petition:

Hallowed be Thy name.
Ps. 8, 15, 16, 50, 52, 68, 76, 78, 80, 83, 86, 89, 95, 96, 105, 106, 115, 124, 135, 138, 145, 148

(Faith and life in God's name)

Second Petition:

Thy kingdom come.
Ps. 1, 2, 14, 17, 18, 21, 24, 37, 40, 43, 44, 45, 46, 47, 48, 53, 57, 58, 60, 61, 65, 72, 74, 82, 87, 93, 97, 110, 125, 126, 127, 132, 147

(Hearing and keeping God's Word)

---

1   Dietrich Bonhoeffer, "Life Together," in *Dietrich Bonhoeffer's Works* 5, trans. Daniel W. Bloesch and James H. Burtness, ed. Geffrey B. Kelly (Minneapolis: Fortress, 1996), 58.

Third Petition:

Thy will be done on earth as it is in heaven.
Ps. 19, 33, 41, 49, 62, 63, 66, 67, 71, 73, 77,
81, 85, 92, 94, 101, 108, in heaven 112, 114,
119, 122, 128, 129, 133, 134, 137, 144

(Strengthening of faith; trust in God's good will)

Fourth Petition:

Give us this day our daily bread.
Ps. 20, 75, 100, 103, 104, 107, 111, 136

(Thanksgiving)

Fifth Petition:

***And forgive us our trespasses as we
forgive those who trespass against us.***
Ps. 6, 32, 38, 51, 102, 130, 143

(Confession and Absolution)

Sixth Petition:

And lead us not into temptation.
Ps. 7, 13, 26, 91, 139, 141, 142, 146

(In times of temptation)

Seventh Petition:

But deliver us from evil.
Ps. 3, 4, 5, 10, 11, 12, 25, 28, 30, 31, 35, 36, 38, 39, 54,
55, 59, 64, 69, 70, 79, 88, 90, 109, 120, 123, 140, 143

(Healing and protection; confidence in the face of death)

Conclusion:

***For thine is the kingdom and the power and
the glory forever and ever. Amen.***
Ps. 9, 22, 27, 29, 34, 56, 98, 99, 113, 149, 150

(Confidence in Christ, who is the "Amen"
to every promise of God)

APPENDIX IV: PREPARATION FOR CONFESSION AND ABSOLUTION ACCORDING TO THE TEN COMMANDMENTS

"Preparation for Confession and Absolution According to the Ten Commandments" is taken from *Treasury of Daily Prayer.*[1] This devotional piece uses the Ten Commandments as a "confessional mirror" in a manner suggested by Luther in his 1522 *Personal Prayer Book*, where the reformer gives examples of how each commandment is either broken or fulfilled.[2] "Preparation for Confession and Absolution According to the Ten Commandments" provides Christians with a tool for a reflective praying of the Commandments with the confession of sins in view.

The First Commandment
You shall have no other gods.

What does this mean?
We should fear, love, and trust in God above all things.

What or whom do I fear most?

In what or whom do I trust most for financial security, physical safety, or emotional support?

Do I fear God's wrath and therefore avoid every sin?

Is my love of God evident in my daily life?

Do I expect only good from God in every situation, or do I worry, doubt, complain, or feel unfairly treated when things go wrong?

---

1   *Treasury of Daily Prayer*, gen. ed. Scot A. Kinnaman (St. Louis: Concordia, 2008), 1460–62.

2   AE 43:17–24.

The Second Commandment
You shall not misuse the name of the Lord your God.

What does this mean?
We should fear and love God so that we do not curse,
swear, use satanic arts, lie, or deceive by His name, but call
upon it in every trouble, pray, praise, and give thanks.

Does the Gospel adorn my daily speech and conduct, or do I curse,
speak carelessly, or misuse God's name?

Have I kept all the vows I have made in the Lord's name?

Am I diligent and sincere in my prayers, or have I been lazy, bored, or
distracted? Do I trust that the Lord God will answer them according
to His good and gracious will?

The Third Commandment
Remember the Sabbath day by keeping it holy.

What does this mean?
We should fear and love God so that we do not despise preaching
and His Word, but hold it sacred and gladly hear and learn it.

Do I despise the Word by neglect or by paying little or no attention
when it is read or preached?

Am I faithful in the Divine Service, or do I attend sporadically, prefer-
ring to be elsewhere when the Church is at worship?

Do I pray for my pastor and support his efforts to guard Christ's flock
from error?

The Fourth Commandment
Honor your father and your mother.

What does this mean?
We should fear and love God so that we do not despise
or anger our parents and other authorities, but honor
them, serve and obey them, love and cherish them.

Do I submit to those whom God has put in authority over me?

Have I been ashamed of, angry, stubborn, or disrespectful toward my parents, teachers, employer, pastor, government, or other authorities?

Do I obey all the laws of the city, state, and country, and pay my rightful share of all taxes?

The Fifth Commandment
You shall not murder.

What does this mean?
We should fear and love God so that we do not
hurt or harm our neighbor in his body, but help
and support him in every physical need.

Have I unjustly taken the life of anyone, born or unborn?

Do I hate anyone, or am I angry with anyone?

Do I hold grudges or harbor resentment?

Am I abusive (in word or deed) toward my spouse, children, or anyone else?

Have I ignored the plight of the helpless or been callous toward genuine need?

The Sixth Commandment
You shall not commit adultery.

What does this mean?
We should fear and love God so that we lead a sexually
pure and decent life in what we say and do, and
husband and wife love and honor each other.

Have I held in highest regard God's gift of sexuality or have I debased
it in any way by my thoughts, words or conduct?

Am I guilty of lust, indecency, or the use of pornography?

Have I reserved my sexual activity for the pleasure and consolation of
my spouse, and when God wills, the procreation of children?

The Seventh Commandment
You shall not steal.

What does this mean?
We should fear and love God so that we do not take
our neighbor's money or possessions, or get them
in any dishonest way, but help him to improve
and protect his possessions and income.

Have I gotten anything in a dishonest way?

Have I made illegal copies of any printed material, audio or video
tapes, or computer programs?

Do I faithfully attend to the responsibilities of my vocation?

Do I take care of what I have, pay what I owe, return what I borrow,
and respect other people's property?

Do I give generously, or am I selfish, stingy, and greedy with my time
and money?

The Eighth Commandment
You shall not give false testimony against your neighbor.

What does this mean?
We should fear and love God so that we do not tell
lies about our neighbor, betray him, slander him, or
hurt his reputation, but defend him, speak well of
him, and explain everything in the kindest way.

Do I speak the truth or have I lied in any way?

Do I gossip or take pleasure in talking about the faults and mistakes of
others?

Do I uphold and defend the name and reputation of others?

Have I judged others without being duly authorized to do so?

Have I gladly and willingly found ways to explain in the best possible
way the words or actions of those who hurt me?

Am I the first to admit my own mistakes, or do I cover up my sins and
make myself look better than I am?

The Ninth Commandment
You shall not covet your neighbor's house.

What does this mean?
We should fear and love God so that we do not scheme to get
our neighbor's inheritance or house, or get it in a way which only
appears right, but help and be of service to him in keeping it.

Do I have strong wants, desires, or cravings that consume my thoughts?

Do I resent or envy those who have more than I?

Do I neglect my marriage, family, church, and other relationships in a
desperate attempt to satisfy the wants and desires of my flesh?

Have my wants kept me from being happy with and thankful for what God has given me?

The Tenth Commandment

You shall not covet your neighbor's wife, or his manservant or maidservant, his ox or donkey, or anything that belongs to your neighbor.

What does this mean?

We should fear and love God so that we do not entice or force away our neighbor's wife, workers, or animals, or turn them against him, but urge them to stay and do their duty.

Am I discontented with the spouse the Lord God has given me?

Am I discontented with the job I have or the employees I supervise?

Have I neglected to urge someone to remain faithful to his or her spouse?

Have I wanted my neighbor's husband or wife, boyfriend or girl-friend, workers or property to be mine?

Bibliography for
Further Reading and Study

This bibliography of secondary literature, for the most part, represents scholarly work done on Luther's catechisms in the last several decades. My work in this volume has been largely dependent on the research of Oswald Bayer, Robert Kolb, Herbert Girgensohn, and most especially the stellar, five-volume commentary by Albrecht Peters. This bibliography will guide interested readers deeper into the current literature not only of these authors but also of other significant theologians whose work has significantly contributed to our understanding and use of the catechisms.

Althaus, Paul. *The Ethics of Martin Luther*. Translated by Robert C. Schultz. Philadelphia: Fortress, 1972.

———. *Thou Shalt! Sermons Based on the Ten Commandments*. Translated by John W. Rilling. Springfield, OH: Chantry Music Press, 1971.

Arand, Charles. "Catechismal Services: A Bridge Between Evangelism and Assimilation." *Concordia Journal* (July 1997): 177–91.

———. "Luther on the God Behind the First Commandment." *Lutheran Quarterly* 8 (Winter 1994): 395–422.

———. *That I May Be His Own: An Overview of Luther's Catechisms*. St. Louis: Concordia, 2000.

———, Robert Kolb, and James A. Nestingen. *The Lutheran Confessions: History and Theology of the Book of Concord*. Minneapolis: Fortress, 2012.

Baker, Robert, ed. *Lutheran Spirituality: Life as God's Child*. St. Louis: Concordia, 2010.

Bast, Robert James. *Honor Your Fathers: Catechisms and the Emergence of a Patriarchal Ideology in Germany, 1400–1600*. Leiden: Brill, 1997.

Bayer, Oswald. "God's Omnipotence." *Lutheran Quarterly* 23 (Spring 2009): 85–102.

———. "I Believe That God Has Created Me with All That Exists:—An Example of Catecheti-cal-Systematics." *Lutheran Quarterly* 8 (Summer 1994): 129–61.

———. *Living by Faith.* Translated by Geoffrey W. Bromiley. Grand Rapids: Eerdmans, 2003.

———. "Luther's View of Marriage." Pages 169–82 in *Freedom in Response: Lutheran Ethics: Sources and Controversies.* Translated by Jeffrey Cayzer. Oxford: Oxford University Press, 2007.

———. "Martin Luther." Pages 51–66 in *The Reformation Theologians.* Edited by Carter Lindberg. Malden, MA: Blackwell, 2002.

———. *Martin Luther's Theology: A Contemporary Interpretation.* Translated by Thomas H. Trapp. Grand Rapids: Eerdmans, 2008.

———. "Nature and Institution: Luther's Doctrine of the Three Estates." Pages 90–118 in *Freedom in Response: Lutheran Ethics: Sources and Controversies.* Translated by Jeffrey Cayzer. Oxford: Oxford University Press, 2007.

———. "The Doctrine of Justification and Ontology." *Neue Zeitschrift für Systematische Theologie und Religionsphilosphie* 43, no. 1 (2001): 44–53.

———. "The Plurality of the One God and the Plurality of the Gods." *Pro Ecclesia* 25, no. 3 (Summer 2006): 338–54.

———. *Theology the Lutheran Way.* Translated by Jeffrey Silcock and Mark Mattes. Grand Rapids: Eerdmans, 2007.

Bender, Peter. *Lutheran Catechesis.* 2nd edition. Sussex, WI: Concordia Catechetical Academy, 2008.

Bode, Gerhard. "Instruction of the Christian Faith by Lutherans after Luther." Pages 159–204 in *Lutheran Ecclesiastical Culture, 1550–1675.* Edited by Robert Kolb. Leiden: Brill, 2008.

Bonhoeffer, Dietrich. *Psalms: The Prayer Book of the Bible.* Translated by James Burtness. Minneapolis: Augsburg, 1970.

Bornkamm, Heinrich. *Luther in Mid-Career, 1521–1530.* Edited by Karin Bornkamm. Translated by E. Theodore Bachmann. Minneapolis: Fortress, 1983.

Brecht, Martin. *Martin Luther: The Preservation of the Church, 1532–1546.* Translated by James L. Schaaf. Minneapolis: Fortress, 1993.

Brown, Christopher Boyd. "Devotional Life in Hymns, Liturgy, Music, and Prayer." Pages 250–58 in *Lutheran Ecclesiastical Culture, 1550–1675.* Edited by Robert Kolb. Leiden: Brill, 2008.

———. *Singing the Gospel: Lutheran Hymns and the Success of the Reformation.* Harvard Historical Studies 148. Cambridge, MA: Harvard University Press, 2005.

Brunner, Peter. "Salvation and the Office of the Ministry." *Lutheran Quarterly* 15, no. 2 (May 1963): 99–117.

Ebeling, Gerhard. *Luther: An Introduction to His Thought.* Translated by R. A. Wilson. Philadelphia: Fortress, 1972.

Eichrodt, Walter. *Theology of the Old Testament.* Translated by J. A. Baker. Philadelphia: Westminster Press, 1961.

Elert, Werner. *Last Things.* Edited by Rudolph F. Norden. Translated by Martin Bertram. St. Louis: Concordia, 1974.

———. *The Christian Ethos.* Translated by Carl J. Schindler. Philadelphia: Fortress, 1957.

———. *The Structure of Lutheranism.* Translated by Walter A. Hansen. St. Louis: Concordia, 1962.

Fagerberg, Holsten. *A New Look at the Lutheran Confessions (1529–1537).* Translated by Gene J. Lund. St. Louis: Concordia, 1972.

Girgensohn, Herbert. *Teaching Luther's Catechisms.* Translated by John Doberstein. 2 volumes. Philadelphia: Muhlenberg Press, 1959.

Goppelt, Leonhard. *A Commentary on 1 Peter.* Translated by John E. Alsup. Grand Rapids: Eerdmans, 1993.

Grane, Leif. *The Augsburg Confession: A Commentary*. Translated by John Rasmussen. Minneapolis: Augsburg, 1987.

Haemig, Mary Jane. "Preaching the Catechism: A Transformational Enterprise." *Dialog* 36 (1997): 133–45.

Hamm, Berndt. *The Early Luther: Stages in Reformation Reorientation*. Translated by Martin J. Lohrmann. Grand Rapids: Eerdmans, 2014.

Härle, Wilfried. *Outline of Christian Doctrine*. Translated by Ruth Yule and Nicholas Sagovsky. Grand Rapids: Eerdmans, 2015.

Harran, Marilyn J. *Martin Luther: Learning for Life*. St. Louis: Concordia, 1997.

Hinckley, Robert. "Andreas Osiander and the Fifth Chief Part." *Logia* 10, no. 4 (Reformation 2001): 37–42.

Hunnius, Aegidius. *The Christian Table of Duties (1588)*. Translated by Paul A. Rydecki. Malone, TX: Repristination Press, 2013.

Iwand, Hans Joachim. "Die Predigt des Gesetzes." In *Glaubensgerechtigkeit: Gesammelte Aufsätze*. Volume 2. Edited by Gerhard Sauter. Munich: Christian Kaiser, 1980.

———. *The Righteousness of Faith according to Luther*. Edited by Virgil F. Thompson. Translated by Randi H. Lundell. Eugene, OR: Wipf & Stock, 2008.

Janz, Denis. *Three Reformation Catechisms: Catholic, Anabaptist, Lutheran*. New York: Edwin Mellen Press, 1982.

Jensen, Gordon. "Luther and the Lord's Supper." Pages 322–31 in *The Oxford Handbook of Martin Luther's Theology*. Edited by Robert Kolb, Irene Dingel, L'ubomír Batka. Oxford: Oxford University Press, 2014.

Jüngel, Eberhard. *The Freedom of a Christian: Luther's Significance for Contemporary Theology*. Translated by Roy A. Harrisville. Minneapolis: Augsburg, 1988.

Kinnaman, Scot A., gen. ed. *A Treasury of Daily Prayer*. St. Louis: Concordia, 2008.

Klän, Werner. "The 'Third Sacrament': Confession and Repentance in the Confessions of the Lutheran Church." Translated by Mathias Hohls. *Logia* 20, no. 3 (Holy Trinity 2011).

Klug, Eugene F., trans. and ed. *Sermons of Martin Luther: The House Postils*. 3 volumes. Grand Rapids: Baker, 1996.

Kolb, Robert. *Luther and the Stories of God: Biblical Narratives for Christian Living*. Grand Rapids: Baker Academic, 2012.

————. "The Lutheran Doctrine of Original Sin." Pages 109–28 in *Adam, the Fall, and Original Sin: Theological, Biblical, and Scientific Perspectives*. Edited by Hans Madueme and Michael Reeves. Grand Rapids: Baker Academic, 2014.

————. *Martin Luther: Confessor of the Faith*. Oxford: Oxford University Press, 2009.

————, and James A. Nestingen. *Sources and Contexts of the Book of Concord*. Minneapolis: Fortress, 2001.

————. "What Benefit Does the Soul Receive from a Handful of Water? Luther's Preaching on Baptism, 1528–1539." In *Luther's Way of Thinking: Introductory Essays*. Trivandrum, India: Luther Academy India, 2006.

————. *Teaching God's Children His Teaching: A Guide for the Study of Luther's Catechism*. Indian Edition. St. Louis: Luther Academy, 2004.

————, and Timothy Wengert, eds. *The Book of Concord*. Minneapolis: Fortress, 2000.

Korby, Kenneth F. "Prayer: Pre-Reformation to the Present." In *Christians at Prayer*. Edited by John Gallen, S.J. Notre Dame, IN: University of Notre Dame Press, 1977.

————. "The Use of John 6 in Lutheran Sacramental Piety." In *Shepherd the Church: Essays in Honor of the Rev. Dr. Roger D. Pittelko*. Edited by Frederic Baue et al. Fort Wayne, IN: Concordia Theological Seminary Press, 2002.

Korcok, Thomas. *Lutheran Education: From Wittenberg to the Future*. St. Louis: Concordia, 2011.

Kraus, Hans-Joachim. *Psalms 1–59: A Continental Commentary*. Translated by Hilton C. Oswald. Minneapolis: Fortress, 1993.

———. *Theology of the Psalms*. Translated by Keith Crim. Minneapolis: Fortress, 1992.

Krause, Richard A. "Remember the Saxon Visitation: Devotional Modeling for Christian Families." *Logia* 16, no. 4 (Reformation 2007): 21–28.

Krodel, Gottfried. "Luther as a Creative Writer: The Explanation of the Second Article of the Apostles' Creed in the Small Catechism." In *Ad Fontes Lutheri: Toward the Recovery of the Real Luther: Essays in Honor of Kenneth Hagen's Sixty-Fifth Birthday.* Edited by Timothy Maschke et al. Milwaukee: Marquette University Press, 2001.

———. "Luther's Work on the Catechism in the Context of Late Medieval Catechetical Literature." *Concordia Journal* 25, no. 4 (October 1999): 364–404.

Lazareth, William. *Luther on the Christian Home.* Philadelphia: Muhlenberg Press, 1960.

Leaver, Robin. "Luther's Catechism Hymns 2: Ten Commandments." *Lutheran Quarterly* 11 (Winter 1997): 411–21.

———. *Luther's Liturgical Music: Principles and Implications*. Grand Rapids: Eerdmans, 2007.

Lehmann, Martin E. *Luther and Prayer.* Milwaukee: Northwestern, 1985.

Lindberg, Carter. "Piety, Prayer, and Worship in Luther's View of Daily Life." Pages 414–26 in *The Oxford Handbook of Martin Luther's Theology*. Edited by Robert Kolb, Irene Dingel, L'ubomír Batka. Oxford: Oxford University Press, 2014.

———. "The Future of a Tradition: Luther and the Family." In *All Theology Is Christology: Essays in Honor of David P. Scaer*. Edited by Dean Wenthe et al. Fort Wayne, IN: Concordia Theological Seminary Press, 2000, 133.

Loewenich, Walther von. *Luther's Theology of the Cross*. Translated by Herbert J. A. Bouman. Minneapolis: Augsburg, 1976.

Löhe, Wilhelm. *Three Books about the Church*. Translated and edited by James L. Schaaf. Philadelphia: Fortress, 1969.

Lohmeyer, Ernst. *"Our Father": An Introduction to the Lord's Prayer*. Translated by John Bowden. New York: Harper & Row, 1965.

Lohse, Bernhard. *Martin Luther's Theology: Its Historical and Systematic Development*. Translated by Roy A. Harrisville. Minneapolis: Fortress, 1999.

Ludwig, Alan. "Preaching and Teaching the Creed: The Structures of the Small Catechism's Explanations as Guides." *Logia* 3, no. 4 (Reformation 1994): 11–24.

Mattes, Mark. "Discipleship in Lutheran Perspective." *Lutheran Quarterly* 26 (Summer 2012): 142–63.

Maxfield, John A. "Martin Luther and Idolatry." Pages 141–68 in *The Reformation as Christianization: Essays on Scott Hendrix's Christianization Thesis*. Edited by Anna Marie Johnson and John A. Maxfield. Tübingen: Mohr Siebeck, 2012.

McNair, Bruce G. "Luther and the Pastoral Theology of the Lord's Prayer." *Logia* 14, no. 4 (Reformation 2005).

Mildenberger, Friedrich. *Theology of the Lutheran Confessions*. Edited by Robert C. Schultz. Translated by Erwin Lueker. Philadelphia: Fortress, 1986.

Nestingen, James A. "Luther's Cultural Translation of the Catechism." *Lutheran Quarterly* 15 (Winter 2001): 440–52.

———. *Martin Luther: A Life*. Minneapolis: Augsburg Fortress, 2003.

———. "Preaching the Catechism." *Word & World* 10, no. 1 (Winter 1990): 33–42.

———. "The Catechism's *Simul*." *Word & World* 3, no. 4 (Fall 1983): 364–72.

———. "The Lord's Prayer in Luther's Catechism." *Word & World* 22, no. 1 (Winter 2002): 36–48.

Noll, Mark A. *Confessions and Catechisms of the Reformation.* Vancouver: Regent College Press, 2004.

Nordling, John. "The Catechism: The Heart of the Reformation." *Logia* 16, no. 4 (Reformation 2007): 5–14.

Olson, Oliver K. *Reclaiming Lutheran Confirmation.* Minneapolis: Lutheran Press, 2015.

Ozment, Steven. *When Fathers Ruled: Family Life in Reformation Europe.* Cambridge, MA: Harvard University Press, 1983.

Parsons, Michael. *Reformation Marriage: The Husband and Wife Relationship in the Theology of Luther and Calvin.* Edinburgh: Rutherford House, 2005.

Paulson, Steven. "Graspable God." *Word & World* 32, no. 1 (Winter 2012): 51–62.

———. *Lutheran Theology.* London: T&T Clark, 2011.

Peters, Albrecht. *Baptism and Lord's Supper*. Translated by Thomas H. Trapp. Commentary on Luther's Catechisms 4. St. Louis: Concordia, 2012.

———. *Confession and Christian Life.* Translated by Thomas H. Trapp. Commentary on Luther's Catechisms 5. St. Louis: Concordia, 2013.

———. *Creed.* Translated by Thomas H. Trapp. Commentary on Luther's Catechisms 2. St. Louis: Concordia, 2011.

———. *Lord's Prayer.* Translated by Daniel Thies. Commentary on Luther's Catechisms 3. St. Louis: Concordia, 2011.

———. *Ten Commandments.* Translated by Holger Sonntag. Commentary on Luther's Catechisms 1. St. Louis: Concordia, 2009.

Pinomaa, Lennart. *Faith Victorious: An Introduction to Luther's Theology*. Translated by Walter J. Kukkonen. Philadelphia: Fortress, 1963.

Pless, John T. *A Small Catechism on Human Life.* St. Louis: LCMS World Relief & Human Care, 2006.

————. "Catechesis for Life in the Royal Priesthood." In *A Reader in Pastoral Theology*. Edited by John T. Pless. Fort Wayne, IN: Concordia Theological Seminary Press, 2002.

————. "Catechism Foundations." Pages 33–44 in *Confirmation Basics*. Edited by Mark Sengele. St. Louis: Concordia, 2009.

————. "Ceremonies for Seekers: Catechesis as a Fundamental Criterion for Worship in the Lutheran Confessions." In *Worship 2000*. Edited by John and Jennifer Maxfield. St. Louis: Luther Academy, 2010.

————. *Didache*. Fort Wayne, IN: Emmanuel Press, 2013.

————. "Fidelity to the Catechism in Prayer and Teaching." *Lutheran Forum* (Fall 2005): 8–15.

————. *Handling the Word of Truth: Law and Gospel in the Church Today*. St. Louis: Concordia, 2004.

————. *Martin Luther: Preacher of the Cross—A Study in Luther's Pastoral Theology*. St. Louis: Concordia, 2013.

————. "Preaching the Catechism—Part I." *Concordia Pulpit Resources* (May 30–August 29, 2010): 3–8.

————. "Preaching the Catechism—Part II." *Concordia Pulpit Resources* (September 5–November 21, 2010): 3–6.

————. "The Catechism as the Handbook for the Vocation of the Laity in Worship and Prayer." Pages 81–97 in *The Lutheran Doctrine of Vocation*. Edited by John A. Maxfield. St. Louis: Concordia Historical Institute and Luther Academy, 2008.

————. "Reviewing Curriculum." Pages 46–55 in *Sunday School Basics*. Edited by Mark Sengele. St. Louis: Concordia, 2005.

Rad, Gerhard von. *Old Testament Theology*. Translated by D. M. G Stalker. New York: Harper & Row, 1962.

Reu, J. Michel. *Catechetics*. Chicago: Wartburg, 1927.

Rittgers, Ronald K. "Private Confession in the German Reformation." Pages 189–207 in *Repentance in Christian Theology*. Edited by Mark J. Boda and Gordon T. Smith. Collegeville, MN: Liturgical Press, 2006.

———. *The Reformation of the Keys: Confession, Conscience, and Authority in Sixteenth-Century Germany*. Cambridge, MA: Harvard University Press, 2004.

Russell, William R. *Praying for Reform: Martin Luther, Prayer, and the Christian Life*. Minneapolis: Augsburg Fortress, 2005.

Saainen, Risto. "Luther and *Beneficia*." Pages 169–88 in *The Reformation as Christianization: Essays on Scott Hendrix's Christianization Thesis*. Edited by Anna Marie Johnson and John A. Maxfield. Tübingen: Mohr Siebeck, 2012.

Sasse, Hermann. *Here We Stand*. Translated by Theodore G. Tappert. Adelaide, Australia: Lutheran Publishing House, 1979.

———. "Holy Baptism." Translated by Norman Nagel. Pages 56–67 in volume 1 of *Letters to Lutheran Pastors*. Edited by Matthew C. Harrison. St. Louis: Concordia, 2013.

———. "Jesus Christ Is Lord: The Church's Original Confession." In *We Confess: Jesus Christ*. Translated by Norman E. Nagel. St. Louis: Concordia, 1984.

———. *We Confess: Jesus Christ*. Translated by Norman E. Nagel. St. Louis: Concordia, 1984.

Schild, Maurice. "Praying the Catechism and Defrocking the Devil: Aspects of Luther's Spirituality." *Lutheran Theological Journal* 10, no. 2 (August 1976): 48–56.

Schlink, Edmund. *The Doctrine of Baptism*. Translated by Herbert J. A. Bouman. St. Louis: Concordia, 1972.

———. *Theology of the Lutheran Confessions*. Translated by Paul F. Koehneke and Herbert J. A. Bouman. St. Louis: Concordia, 2003.

Schnelle, Udo. *Apostle Paul: His Life and Theology*. Translated by M. Eugene Boring. Grand Rapids: Baker Academic, 2005.

———. *Theology of the New Testament*. Translated by M. Eugene Boring. Grand Rapids: Baker Academic, 2009.

Schulz, Frieder. "Luther's Household Prayers." Pages 235–51 in Albrecht Peters, *Confession and Christian Life*. Translated by Thomas H. Trapp. St. Louis: Concordia, 2013.

Schulz, Robert C. "The Theological Significance of the Order of the Chief Parts in Luther's Catechism." In *Teaching the Faith: Luther's Catechisms in Perspective*. Edited by Carl A. Volz. River Forest, IL: Lutheran Education Association, 1967.

Schwarz, Hans. *The Human Being: A Theological Anthropology*. Grand Rapids: Eerdmans, 2013.

Schwarz, Reinhard. "The Last Supper: The Testament of Jesus." *Lutheran Quarterly* 9 (Winter 1995): 391–404.

Schwarzwäller, Klaus. *Cross and Resurrection: God's Wonder and Mystery*. Translated by Mark Mattes and Ken Sundet Jones. Minneapolis: Fortress, 2012.

Seifrid, Mark. "Romans 7: The Voice of the Law, the Cry of Lament, and the Shout of Thanksgiving." Pages 111–65 in *Perspectives on Our Struggle with Sin: 3 Views of Romans 7*. Edited by Terry L. Wilder. Nashville: B&H Academic, 2011.

Siggins, Ian. *Martin Luther's Doctrine of Christ*. New Haven: Yale University Press, 1970.

Silcock, Jeffrey. "Luther on the Holy Spirit and His Use of God's Word." Pages 294–309 in *The Oxford Handbook of Martin Luther's Theology*. Edited by Robert Kolb, Irene Dingel, L'ubomír Batka. Oxford: Oxford University Press, 2014.

Slenczka, Reinhard. "Luther's Care of Souls for Our Times." *Concordia Theological Quarterly* 67, no. 1 (January 2003): 33–63.

Spinks, Bryan. *Reformation and Modern Rituals and Theologies of Baptism: From Luther to Contemporary Practices*. Burlington, VT: Ashgate, 2006.

Steinmetz, David. "Luther and Formation in Faith." Pages 253–69 in *Educating People of Faith*. Edited by John Van Engen. Grand Rapids: Eerdmans, 2004.

Tappert, Theodore G., trans. and ed. *Luther: Letters of Spiritual Counsel*. Philadelphia: Westminster, 1955.

Thielicke, Helmut. *The Evangelical Faith*. Translated by Geoffrey W. Bromiley. Grand Rapids: Eerdmans, 1982.

Thompson, Virgil. "The Promise of Catechesis." *Lutheran Quarterly* 4 (Autumn 1990): 259–70.

Trigg, Jonathan. Baptism in the Theology of Martin Luther. Leiden: Brill, 2001.

———. "Luther on Baptism and Penance." Pages 310–21 in *The Oxford Handbook of Martin Luther's Theology*. Edited by Robert Kolb, Irene Dingel, L'ubomír Batka. Oxford: Oxford University Press, 2014.

Trillhaas, Wolfgang. "Regnum Christi: On the History of the Concept in Protestantism." *Lutheran World* 14 (1967).

Truebenbach, Kim A. "Luther's Two Kingdoms in the Third and Fourth Petitions." *Lutheran Quarterly* 24, no. 4 (Winter 2010): 469–73.

Vajta, Vilmos. *Luther on Worship*. Translated by U. S. Leupold. Philadelphia: Muhlenberg, 1958.

Vicedom, Georg. *A Prayer for the World*. Translated by Edward and Marie Schroeder. St. Louis: Concordia, 1967.

Wendebourg, Dorothea. "Luther on Monasticism." *Lutheran Quarterly* 19 (Summer 2005): 125–52.

Wengert, Timothy J. "Fear and Love in the Ten Commandments." *Concordia Journal* 21 (January 1995): 14–27.

———. *Martin Luther's Catechisms: Forming the Faith*. Minneapolis: Fortress, 2009.

———. "Wittenberg's Earliest Catechism." *Lutheran Quarterly* 7 (Autumn 1993): 247–60.

Westermann, Claus. *The Praise of God in the Psalms*. Translated by Keith R. Crim. Richmond: John Knox Press, 1965.

Winger, Thomas. "Order 'in the Lord': Parents/Children, Masters/Slaves." Pages 654–96 in *Ephesians*. Concordia Commentary. St. Louis: Concordia, 2015.

———. "The Gospel in God's Order: The Bridegroom and the Bride." Pages 598–653 in *Ephesians*. Concordia Commentary. St. Louis: Concordia, 2015.

Wingren, Gustaf. *Luther on Vocation*. Translated by Carl C. Rasmussen. Philadelphia: Muhlenberg Press, 1957.

Wisløff, Carl. *The Gift of Communion: Luther's Controversy with Rome on Eucharistic Sacrifice*. Translated by Joseph Shaw. Minneapolis: Augsburg, 1964.

Wolff, Hans Walter. Page 228 in *Anthropology of the Old Testament*. Translated by Margret Kohl. Philadelphia: Fortress, 1974.